The LIFEWORK GUIDE to HAPPINESS

Becoming the person
God
created you to be,
achieving your dreams,
being a becon of light
for the world

CHRISTOPHER M. KASIAN

Copyright © 2014 by Christopher M. Kasian

The Lifework Guide to Happiness
Becoming the person God created you to be, achieving your dreams, being a becon of light for the world
by Christopher M. Kasian

Printed in the United States of America

ISBN 9781629523927

All rights reserved solely by the author. The author guarantees all contents are original and do not infringe upon the legal rights of any other person or work. No part of this book may be reproduced in any form without the permission of the author. The views expressed in this book are not necessarily those of the publisher.

Unless otherwise indicated, Bible quotations are taken from New King James Version®. Copyright © 1982 by Thomas Nelson, Inc. Used by permission. All rights reserved.

www.xulonpress.com

Uncle George,

I want to thank you for being such an influential figure in my life. You're a true role model. I hope when I meet the right woman I can provide for her and our children like you have done. I hope you and the family find this read to make you think, smile, cry and see the glory of God. May God continue to bless you and the family!

- as ever, love,

Christopher

TABLE OF CONTENTS

Introduction ix

Journey, Not a Destination xi

Chapter 1: Mom: 13
   Love your Family and Country, Self Discipline
   is the Greatest Achievement

Chapter 2: Dad: 21
   Enjoy What You Do No Matter What You Do, Reading is Your
   Best Friend

Chapter 3: Gramp Kasian: 28
   Smile

Chapter 4: Gram Kasian: 33
   Believe in the People Who Believe in You

Chapter 5: Gram Cibik: 38
   Prayer is the Most Powerful Thing in the World

Chapter 6: Uncle Andy: 42
   Do Things Your Way

Chapter 7: Uncle Franky: 46
   When You Rush, Accidents Happen

Chapter 8: Joe Grella: 51
   "Get the Roots!"

Chapter 9: Coach Jim Stone: 55
   Working to Win Is Everything

Chapter 10: Mr. Litchkofski: 62
   Don't Ever Change

Chapter 11: Sister Andrea: 67
"Integrity Is to...."

Chapter 12: Coach Teddy Napierkowski: 73
Be Grateful for What You Have, Not Ungrateful for What You Don't Have

Chapter 13: Ed Ackerman: 78
The Greatest Thing You Can Give Someone Is Your Time

Chapter 14: Uncle George: 82
Make the American Dream Live

Chapter 15: Aunt Katie: 87
Your Spouse Is Your Best Friend

Chapter 16: 91
Fatherly Advice

Chapter 17: Fatherly Advice #1: 94
Girls + Guys + Booze + Hormones = TROUBLE

Chapter 18: Fatherly Advice #2: 98
Tell Your Significant Other They Are the Cleanup Hitter

Chapter 19: Fatherly Advice #3: 103
#1 Is the Only Number that Matters

Chapter 20: Fatherly Advice #4: 106
Find a Place Where Your Mind and Heart Intersect

Chapter 21: Fatherly Advice #5: 110
Leave the Baggage Dragging Behind and Move Forward

Chapter 22: Fatherly Advice #6: 114
Analyze, Adapt and Achieve

Chapter 23: Fatherly Advice #7: 116
You Are Blessed to Do Great Things

Chapter 24: Fatherly Advice #8: 119
Love Is the Only Package You Can't Leave Behind

Conclusion: 123
The Beginning Is Near

For my Lord and Savior Jesus Christ—because of your love and grace, you have given me life now and everlasting and saved a mere sinner. For my Mom and Dad who are the greatest teachers a young man could ever have. For my grandfather who always inspired me to write, and my grandmother who always inspired me to dream. For my family and friends whose faith, hope and love I will always cherish. For you, the reader: May the *Lifework Guide to Happiness* be a blessing in your life.

On Eagle's Wings,
Christopher M. Kasian

INTRODUCTION

I'm just a teacher and a former athletic coach, so you may be wondering how the *Lifework Guide to Happiness* got started. For the first time in my life I taught seniors in 2007. This was it. There was no turning back for these kids. They were heading into the real world and hopefully were ready to chase their dreams. I recollected what it was like when I was in their shoes so I put together a little booklet of advice called *Everyman's Guide to Happiness*. It's great to hear back from those kids who I taught British Literature to for only a few short months. Some are doing very well, others took a detour and are trying to find their way back home and sadly some have passed on. I always felt like I wanted to do more with the guide when the time was right.

Well, the time was right in February 2012. I was honored to be coaching high school girls' basketball to many great young ladies. The head coach asked me to be the guest speaker at our girls' basketball banquet. I didn't feel worthy of such an honor and I still don't. I went home and prayed. I realized that God gave me an opportunity to honor his name and try to make a positive difference in the lives of our girls. It was time to revisit *Everyman's Guide to Happiness* and put together something new with the wealth of experiences I've been blessed to have the past few years. As the audience looked at my credentials they were probably wondering why I was the guest speaker. I never scored a thousand points, a game winning touchdown, or was honored as an All Scholastic Athlete, so I couldn't really talk about achieving athletic honors in high school and beyond. So what was I going to talk about? As I reflected on what to tell the girls, I was drawn back to what mattered the most. It wasn't a sport or a game. It was the family, many friends, teachers and coaches I've been blessed to know and who had a huge impact on my life. It was the life experiences, detours and failures along the way. It was the Lord picking me up even when I didn't have the strength to crawl. It has been an honor to be a part of so many wonderful people and experiences. They are the clay that has helped mold me into the man I am today. I'm only a teacher and a former coach trying my best to carry on their lessons. I pray every day that I honor them for my students. I pray that their lessons and the experiences along the way will warm your heart and lead you to teach others. The teaching goes on. Pay it forward.

JOURNEY, NOT A DESTINATION

This journey begins with the lifework assignment. There is no earthly destination in sight. The only destination we should all be striving for is spending eternity with our heavenly Father. Here's how we can get started. First, you need to grab a blank sheet of paper and a crayon. It's really important that you use a crayon and not a pen or pencil. I want you to smell that crayon. I know it sounds kind of unusual especially if someone is looking at you right now as you take a whiff of the color magenta. The importance of using a crayon is to remind you of what it was like to be a young, carefree and an innocent child. We should never lose sight of the joys of being a child. Being forever young is truly a blessing as long as we keep gaining wisdom. Secondly, I want you to trace your hand. Please don't try to trace your writing hand because it will sure be one ugly looking depiction.

This marks the beginning of your lifework journey. You will complete this assignment at the book's end. Keep your crayon and a pen handy for note taking but you will not need to use the hand until we complete reading. For now, you need to start reading. I encourage you to shut off the Iphony, log out of Gossipbook and walk away from the 80 channels with nothing on. I encourage you to find some solitude; a nice quiet place where you can go to be at peace. *The Lifework Guide to Happiness* will have no use if you keep the societal drum beating in your life. If the *Lifework Guide* is going to make a difference in your life, you will need to open up your heart, your mind and your soul. In the Old Testament when Elijah waited for God to speak, he waited through an earthquake, loud thunder and the howling wind. God spoke to Elijah in a whisper. In the New Testament when Jesus talked about praying he urged people to do so alone, in silence, unlike the hypocrites who did so in front of large crowds. I truly believe that this book is in your hands right now because the good Lord wants to speak to you through an ordinary guy like myself. Do you want to know something? He always wants to speak to you. Maybe you've tuned him out and focused more on sports, your boyfriend/girlfriend, the TV, Gossipbook or texting your friends with your Iphony? Maybe you never heard Jesus speak to you before? Only you know the answer to these questions. Do you want to know something else? With Jesus, there's always a clean slate. This is your opportunity to wipe the slate clean with the Lord and allow Him to give you a new beginning. It is my prayer that the Lord will bless you and move your heart to listen. He will speak to you. When God speaks, take good notes. It's a good thing you have your favorite pen and crayon handy. Let the journey begin!

Chapter 1: Mom

LOVE YOUR FAMILY AND COUNTRY SELF-DISCIPLINE IS THE GREATEST ACHIEVEMENT

My mom is a retired Lt. Col. in the United States Army. She joined the army reserves while going to college to become a nurse. On Christmas day, 1990, I celebrated Christmas with my mom and dad at Fort Indiantown Gap. I was nine years old and I didn't know if I'd ever see my mom again as my father and I drove away that winter night. The next day my mom left to defend freedom in the Persian Gulf War. It was in the next couple of months that I would learn the importance of loving your family and country.

Every day when I came home from school I would see the footage of the war on CNN. I remember seeing the sky light up with the green scud missiles of the Iraqi forces as they tried to kill Americans. I remember when a scud missile hit a building of reserve army forces that just arrived in Iraq, killing many of them. My mom and the 300th Field Hospital were in the same building one day earlier before they deployed to set up operations in the desert. On the inside I was a terrified nine-year-old who didn't know if Mom was going to come home. But the love of my family protected me from my fears. They all came together at 36 Tanya Drive: family, friends, and neighbors, to provide their love and support to the husband and son of a soldier at war. I remember when my fourth grade teacher, Mrs. Ross, had the students make a Christmas tree for my mom. The Super Bowl that year between the Giants and Bills is something I'll never forget. Everyone gathered together at the house and continued the great American tradition of watching the biggest sporting event in the world. The memory of Whitney Houston singing "The National Anthem" still gives me the goose bumps. I was so proud to be the son of a solider at war and an American. As the war continued, I began to understand how great America really was.

I learned how cruel of a dictator Saddam Hussein was and the atrocities he committed amongst his people. It was also clear to me that America was a nation free of a dictator and instead ruled by the people. I understood how America was the beacon of freedom for the world. If some big bully like Saddam Hussein threatened innocent people, then they turned to the USA for help. The war came to an end and we were victorious in liberating Kuwait from Saddam Hussein's power grip. I was blessed with the greatest birthday gift ever: my mom coming home from Iraq on my 10th birthday. My father, both grandmothers and my mom's good friend drove together to see my mom for the first time in five months. As we drove to Fort Indiantown Gap I remember my father playing Lee Greenwood's "God Bless the USA" over and over again; that song will never get old. I felt so excited to see my mom. Inside I felt a great sense of pride in being an American and knowing that my mom was one of the many great Americans who risked it all to defend freedom. When she came off the bus I laid my eyes on a hero that was just a mom and just a soldier, but so much more to her son.

Get to Work

The new American family is a trial and error. "Hey, let's see if this works out. We'll date for superficial reasons, have some kids and then get married. If it works out, then great. If it doesn't, then that's no big deal; we'll just get a divorce and do it all over again." The new American family is far from marriage between a man and a woman. If the trend continues a man might walk into a church and try to marry a horse someday. The horse thing might sound odd, but I wouldn't be surprised if it happened in the future. Our family values have deteriorated drastically over the years. The way things are going, it's likely to get worse and the horse thing might become a reality. You won't hear me saying "giddy-up" to that idea.

So, what can we do about it? First, we need to put society's definition of marriage on the permanent backburner and return to God's definition of marriage in Genesis. Next, we must start valuing marriage in reverence towards God. God needs to be at the center of every relationship and in every marriage. God wants you to be fruitful and multiply since we are His greatest creation. He molded us in His image and likeness; and tell your earth-loving friends, who don't get the whole God thing, that they should take an anatomy and physiology class if they don't believe that humans are the greatest creation. Lastly, if you come from a bad home and your mom or dad were absent parents, then learn from your experience and be a better father or mother. Stop playing the victim! It's up to you to stop the trend of poor parenting and alternative lifestyles. Teach your children well.

I was blessed to come from a strong family that valued marriage and understood that a God existed. Hard times really hit home when my mom went to war. Who came to the rescue? The answer: God and the family. Although we were all afraid, we still were able to enjoy our lives knowing the power of prayer and family. It wasn't easy, but we did it. I was still able to do my schoolwork, play basketball and be a happy-go-luckynine-year-old because my family's love of God and each other. By no means am I a math person; you'll hear about my math ineptitude later in the book. However, I do know two solutions to every problem that we will ever face: God and family. Love your family!

America is sick! Our country is turning into an implosion zone. God, family and freedom are on the government's hit list. They haven't assassinated any of our values yet, but the shrapnel is sure causing great damage. When God, family and freedom were on the chopping block for the Founders, they said, "We hold these truths to be self-evident, that all men are created equal, that they are endowed by their Creator with certain unalienable Rights, that among these are Life, Liberty, and the pursuit of Happiness." In order to move forward we must look back at a nation that was created and blessed by God. We need to read the true stories of our founders and the founding documents like *The Declaration of Independence* and the *Constitution*. They gave us the answers and showed us the way. We need to retrace their footsteps and unite together as "one nation under God." It's our time to be the Defending Fathers of the United States of America. In doing so, We the People will receive an intimate feeling of love for America. We will have to hold back tears when we sing "The National Anthem." We will look to the heavens above when "God Bless America" plays. We will stand up when big government tells us to sit down. We will put our lives on the line when this great nation's values are for sale. We will "with a firm reliance on Divine Providence mutually pledge to each other our lives, our fortunes and our sacred honor." Love your country!

Self-Discipline is the Greatest Achievement

I started exercising when I was twelve years old, thanks to my mother. I'd wake up for school, watch the old *Dennis the Menace* reruns, eat my Cookie Crisp and take my Flintstones vitamins.

While I was having fun eating and switching the channels between *Dennis the Menace* and *Sportscenter*, my mom was making a sacrifice by exercising. I honestly cannot recall a morning that my mom didn't exercise. My mom would do intervals on the NordicTrack, bike, and stepper and then finish it off with pushups and sit-ups. She wasn't just taking a mild walk; these were intense, empty-the-tank workouts, every single morning. By the time she was finished she was drenched in sweat. My mom would then eat a healthy breakfast, shower up and be off to work at the Veterans' Hospital. I remember one time when I was in my early twenties and my mom wasn't feeling well. I had no idea what was wrong with her, but I did know that it couldn't be good if it required my father to take her to the emergency room. She arrived home around 1 AM and thankfully it wasn't too serious. Even if it was I don't think my mom would've said anything. I awoke at 5 AM to get ready for work and there was my mom already doing her workout. I heard the quote a few times before, "That which you gaze upon you will become." I agree. By the time I reached the age of twelve all the gazing ignited the beginning of my physical fitness training. I started out doing bicep curls with Campbell soup cans and pushups. The next year my parents bought me a universal workout system capable of exercising every body part. I've been blessed to play baseball, basketball, football and track in high school. Late in life I was a competitive runner and biker. I've also been blessed with the opportunity to coach sports at all levels and really focus on strength and conditioning. Fifteen years later I see the importance of having self-discipline and exercising thanks to my mom.

Get to Work

Working out is hard. I know you want the fifteen minutes abs, the instant weight loss from taking Hydroxycut or the quick bulk up through cycling creatine in your diet. Sadly, many young adults are growing up in the steroid era. They see their role models cheating the system and the system cheating them through handing out only minor infractions. There's a song in the movie *Rocky IV* called, "No Easy Way Out." When it comes to working out, there is no easy way out. I hope and pray you don't take the easy way out even when the worldly view of instant gratification is promoted. The only answer to having a healthy body is self-discipline. The bottom line is that you need to train smart and hard and eat smart and hard. Training smart means that you are dedicated to developing a workout plan, adapting to it and sticking to it. This doesn't mean you workout when you feel like it. Training hard means you empty the tank with every workout. This doesn't mean you go to the gym to socialize. You also need to eat smart and hard. Eating smart involves a well balanced diet of natural foods. Eating smart doesn't mean having a bag of Doritos before bed. To eat hard you need to take in good, healthy protein and carbohydrate sources in order to build muscle and energy. Skipping a meal is not eating hard. Working out wasn't meant to be easy, but it was meant to be worth it. It's hard to think of any other activity that builds self-discipline, self-confidence and a self that you'll be happy to look at in the mirror and your doctor will be happy to see for your next checkup. Here's the secret: self-discipline and self-confidence are contagious. Exercising won't just give you a healthy body and healthy mind. It will help you become a better parent and worker. It will help you accomplish other goals in your life because you will have the self-discipline and confidence to do it even if the world tells you to take the easy way out. **ADD Moment: Speaking of self discipline, do you know that I never once heard my mother use foul language. When I was about twelve years old my mother asked me if I wanted a milkshake. Not even thinking I said, "What the hell, I'll have one." You had to see the look on her face. I thought I was dead meat.** Ultimately, your lifestyle will be encouraging others to up the tempo and start taking better care of themselves. God gave us our earthly bodies. His word tells us that we must treat our bodies as a temple. They can be used to set great examples for others. "That which you gaze upon you will become." Taking great care of our earthly bodies is our way of honoring God. Self-discipline is the greatest achievement.

Chapter 2: Dad

ENJOY WHAT YOU DO, NO MATTER WHAT YOU DO
READING IS YOUR BEST FRIEND

Have you ever seen the commercial for the energizer bunny? My dad is very similar to the energizer bunny. He keeps going and going and going. He just doesn't play the drums. My father fishes in the yard. He goes swimming in his hat and jeans and then lays out in the sun. He hoots and hollers like a cowboy when he cuts the grass. I was at my parents a few weeks ago and my dad was singing while running the sweeper. One time he even drank a bottle of 50/50 soda in church because he had an upset stomach. My mom wasn't too happy about that one. My father has fun no matter what he's doing. Now, the neighbors think he's a little crazy. But after 26 years they've grown used to him. My dad really just enjoys life. I remember one time we were watching "The Marine Biologist" episode of *Seinfeld* for the first time. We almost had to give my father the Heimlich maneuver because he was laughing so hard and almost choked on his potatoes. Don't get me wrong, my dad is also a very hard worker. He shoveled coal and drove heavy equipment at UGI, a power plant, for over thirty years. He's worked harder in one week than I'll ever work in my career as a teacher. The American writer Ralph Waldo Emerson once said, "Nothing great in life was ever achieved without enthusiasm." My dad would always tell me, "You only live once." Emerson and my dad are 100% right and I'm glad he passed that lesson on to his son. I've always tried my best to follow his advice. I had some great summer jobs when I was in high school and college. I worked on the grounds crew for a golf course and I also worked on the back of a garbage truck. I worked really hard, but I also had a great deal of fun with the guys. When we used to cut grass at the country club we would slap each other "high five" and dance around the lawnmowers. We actually had shirts made up and called ourselves "Team Toro," named after the lawnmower brand. When I worked on the garbage truck I would really hustle from one stop to the next. I'd wave at people on the back of the truck. My garbage picking partner and I even rigged a radio to the back of the truck. Those days were great! We worked extremely hard and had a blast during the process. "That which you gaze upon you will become." I'm grateful for a father who showed me the importance of expressing excitement for what you do. Like self-discipline, positive energy is also contagious.

Get to Work

You probably hate doing the dishes, running the sweeper, cutting the grass and taking out the garbage. Think of how we all struggle to do the tasks that seem pointless. Before we even take out the trash our mind is already saying, "Oh, I have to take out the trash now. There's going to be so many bags of garbage and right now the game is on TV. Okay, I'll do it." When we finally take out the trash after complaining for a few minutes we do it with very little energy, thus we feel no sense of pride or accomplishment. Sound familiar? We need to go back to the drawing board and retrain the little person in our minds. It has nothing to do with our physical capabilities and everything to do with the little person's temptation to be like Oscar the Grouch instead of a Tigger. Once we start to think positive then we'll start to act positive. If we get excited to take out the trash then we'll act energetic when we do it, resulting in a job well done. We're not reinventing the wheel here. In fact doing things with joy was well documented over 2,000 years ago when Paul wrote his letter to the Galatians. He talked about one of the gifts of the Holy Spirit being joy. Now he didn't say be joyous when you're only doing things you like to do. The point of this gift was to live in a state of joy and not turn on and off the joy button like an automobile. This is going to take a great deal of self-discipline and practice because we are so used to following society's trend of negative energy and only showing enthusiasm for the things we actually like to do. Let's face it, we Americans are spoiled. A former student of mine told me how excited kids were in Afghanistan when soldiers gave them a pencil and paper. Kids in America would probably say, "Where's my Iphony? What do you want me to do with this?" We need to get back to enjoying the basics again and put our Iphonies down. **ADD Moment: Yes, they're Iphonies because they are phony. Sorry Mr. Jobs. You were certainly an innovator. However, our youth are being exploited by all these devices and they're destroying their social skills and work ethics.** Think about this: if you enjoy doing the things you don't like to do, then you're going to love it when you get the opportunity to do what you desire to do. If you want to get the best out of your time here on earth, and make God and those around you smile, then start to enjoy what you do, no matter what you do.

Reading Is Your Best Friend

The best material possession you can give someone is a book. It educates with life lessons, improves reading and writing skills and taps into your greatest sense, the imagination. I'm grateful to my dad for always buying me books when I was growing up. My father went to school during a time when the struggling students got pushed to the back of the room and earned a decent grade as long as they behaved. My dad was one of those struggling students in the back of the room who got by with a below average education thanks to the public school system. Although I never asked my father why he always bought me books, I can surmise that he just wanted to give me the education he never received. He did. I remember one book my father gave me called *The Winner Within*, by legendary basketball coach Pat Riley. I was thirteen years old reading about the price you needed to pay to earn success in life. The book had many quotes in the margins. Many of them really made an impression, like Yogi Berra's quote, "When you come to a fork in the road, take it." There was one that went straight to my heart and has never left. In the back of the book was a quote from Lee Riley, giving advice to his son, Pat. Mr. Riley told his son, "Every now and then, somewhere, some place, sometime, you are going to have to plant your feet, stand firm, and make a point about who you are and what you believe in. When that time comes, Pat, you simply have to do it." My dad was talking to his thirteen-year-old son through Lee Riley's quote. Little did he know the impact it had on me and still has on me.

One year later I was playing baseball and there was this kid who really talked badly about his girlfriend. He treated her like no young lady should be treated. The young lady happened to be my neighbor. Knowing that she was being treated cruelly I told her about her boyfriend and his intentions. At that time I was working as a janitor. It was nighttime and I was emptying garbage at our church's summer bazaar. The sixteen-year-old and ten of his friends surrounded me. He didn't like what I said to his girlfriend. I knew what was coming. He and his friends were going to bully me. He was going to try to harm me. If I fought back then it would be one against eleven. So, I stood there and took three of his best punches. He hit me in the left cheek, then the right cheek and the third time he cracked me in the nose, breaking it. He was older, bigger and stronger than me and his punches didn't even cause me to flinch. God protects those who stand up for what is right. On that night God certainly protected a fourteen-year-old kid caught in the wrath of a bully and his cronies. God understood that I told the truth and was concerned with the welfare of a young lady. I'm sure many wonder why I didn't fight back. The only logical answer I can give is that God took over that night and sent the Holy Spirit to protect me. I planted my feet, stood firm and stood up for what was right. I may have walked away with a broken nose, but most importantly I walked away with my honor.

Get to Work

When I came home from school I would watch *Growing Pains* followed by *The Cosby Show*. Friday nights at 8 would be *Family Matters* with Steve Erkel. These were good shows filled with family values. They made you laugh, cry and think about being a better person. These shows are extremely rare on cable television today. Watching television makes me sick to my stomach when I see the continued erosion of our once solid family values. If you're trying to live your life the right way then you should be getting an upset stomach, too. Get to work! Turn off the tube, get off of Gossipbook, put your Iphony on silent and take out the Good Book, the Bible. Everything you need to know about the purpose of our lives and how we should be striving to live them was written over 3,000 years ago. The Bible is the truth, word for word, not a myth or a story that is outdated. The word of the Lord was the way, is the way and will always be the way. Will you follow? As a born again Christian I know that reading the Bible fills me with the Holy Spirit. It is my spiritual guide that I need to battle the world every day. It directs me towards other great books that teach me life lessons, expand my reading and writing skills, and empower my creativity. The Bible is the way, the truth and the life. Here's the best part, it's free. There's no monthly installment plan or down payment. You don't need a login or a password to use it. You also will not need a remote control. Jesus Christ already paid the ultimate price; all you have to do is open your heart and believe. In a world filled with darkness, the Bible is the light. Find some solitude and take out the Good Book because reading it will be your best friend.

Chapter 3: Gramp Kasian

SMILE

There's not a week that goes by in my life where I don't think of my grandfather. I know he's looking down and smiling. I'm honored to bear the name Kasian because my gramp smiled the second he saw *The Statue of Liberty* for the first time. If anyone had nothing to smile about it was my grandfather. His mother died when he was an infant. His father took off for America and when my grandfather finally met him, nineteen years later, he really didn't want much to do with his son. The first nineteen years of his life my gramp lived in the Ukraine in a section that was extremely poor and directly affected by the communist takeover of Russia. He left when he was nineteen years old for the land of the free. He could not speak English. He had nothing but the shirt on his back and a burlap sack. But he had a hunger in his heart for freedom. A boat brought him here, but his dreams would take him home. When he saw her golden arch he smiled and never stopped. It was his smile that embraced his newfound freedom. It was his smile that learned the English language. It was his smile that strengthened him to work hard. It was his smile that signed him up to defend freedom in World War II. It was his smile that found my grandmother. It was his smile that raised a son. It was his smile that opened a grocery store in a half of a double block house. It was his smile that provided for his family. It was his smile that helped sick veterans in the VA Hospital and encouraged patriotism as an American Legion Commander. It was his smile that thanked God every day. It his smile that wrote this poem on October 9, 1980:

Smile

Years slowly moving past,
like a lovely flower.
Our life will never last.
Who will live tomorrow?

Accept everyone's smile.
Smile, smile in return.
We are here for awhile,
on this earth under the sun.

Smile, smile all you can.
Wish a very nice day,
to some lonely man.
For your kindness he will pray.

Somehow, somewhere slow,

our years are fleeing away.

From young to old we grow.

Let's smile and smile all the way.

Enjoy heavenly raindrops,

birds and leaves on the tree.

Very soon the clock will stop,

for you my dear friend and me.

Get to Work

A smile cannot cure the common cold, change the score on a failing test or heal a broken heart. Here's the key: it sure can help. My grandfather helped many people, during tough times, with his pleasant personality. I'm sure you can recall a time in your life when a smile uplifted your day. I was living in Surfside Beach, South Carolina, during the summer of my senior year of college with a friend. I always dreamed of living at the beach. I'm a beach bum. I had it made. I worked third shift, 11 PM to 7 AM, as a security guard at Broadway at the Beach. I'd come home from work, have a protein shake, watch Sportscenter, then go to bed. I'd wake up at 2 in the afternoon, eat breakfast, and then go to the beach for two hours. I'd go workout, eat my dinner, and then go to work. I was living the dream as a college senior. Well, for about a week in late June the weather got really miserable. It was cloudy with a mild temperature and it just rained. I was really bummed out. I just moped around and felt sorry for myself. I'd say, "God, come on here, cut me a break. I'll never live at the beach again. Can't you just make the weather nice for me?" He didn't and I still moped around. I was moping around on a rainy Monday morning, my day off, when I decided to go to BiLo for groceries. I was at the checkout counter with my usual 20 yogurts, chicken and Chunky Soup when I noticed the bagger. He was an old, hunched over man that just looked tired and lonely. I stopped in my tracks and just pitied this man. As I came closer to him his eyes met mine and he just smiled. He went from a tired, lonely old man to the happiest face I saw in a while. He asked me how I was doing and he told me to have a great day. The whole time he just smiled. I'll never forget the bagger at BiLo that changed my life on a rainy day. I went back to the apartment that day, unpacked my groceries and told myself that I needed to stop slouching around. I went to the library and took out two books, *A Street Car Named Desire* and *The Greatest Speeches of the 20th Century*. On my day off I sat on the porch during the rain and I read two great books. Guess what happened the next day? The rain stopped and the sun came out after a brief vacation. God is good! When I reflect on that old man working at the grocery store I can't help but to think of Jesus. I'm not an expert, but I would have to say that Jesus probably smiled a great deal. After all, do you think he would attract the attention of many people, especially children, if he had a grimace on his face? I can just imagine Jesus walking the streets of Jerusalem, just smiling at everybody. You can call me crazy, but I think Jesus was a smiling kind of guy. My advice to you is to smile. My advice to you is that the sun shines, even on rainy days. You could be the sunshine in someone's rainy day, week, year, or life. Just smile!

Chapter 4: Gram Kasian

BELIEVE IN THE PEOPLE WHO BELIEVE IN YOU

Do you know what the best part of my week is? Visiting my Gram Kasian in the nursing home. She is without a doubt the love of my life. My gram is the most compassionate and faithful woman I've ever met. She always, and I mean always, put others before herself. My gram was not a certified nurse, but she nursed her husband, two sisters, two brother-in-laws and a neighbor for years while they battled death. That's what I call unconditional love. As a young kid and then a young adult lacking confidence, my gram always believed in me. She would always tell me that I could do anything I wanted to as long as I put my mind to it. She believed in me when I had no reason to believe in myself and neither did anybody else.

God blessed me as an athlete. My father would always tell me from the time I was a young boy and first started playing sports that I was a natural. I thank God that he has blessed me with athletic gifts and has given me the opportunity to compete into my early thirties and help others through my talents. I loved playing Little League baseball. Those years contain some of the fondest memories of my life. I was a very good player in Little League. I was on a great team with great coaches in the minor league. This was well before coach pitch or machine pitch. The players pitched and there were no walks. I could throw really hard for my age but I just had a tough time finding the plate. I remember one time I threw forty-six balls to a batter. That was a tough game against the Cubs. The Cubs were the team we were competing with to win the championship. The toughest thing about that game was the way the opposing coach treated me when I was struggling. He laughed at me so everyone could hear and he continued to behave in an unsportsmanlike manner. His actions incited the players and the fans. There I am, a nine-year-old kid who's just trying my best to throw strikes while the opposing coaches, players and fans are trying to make me feel worthless. Guess what? They did make me feel like I was just no good. I went to the dugout after surviving the inning and I just wanted to curl up in a ball and cry. One person wouldn't let that happen: my gram. She grabbed me by the arm and said, "Go out there and show them you're a Kasian." I did. As the season came to an end it was between the Phillies and the Cubs for the championship. Guess who won? We did. Guess who pitched? I did.

Get to Work

Society is turning to collective salvation instead of individual responsibility. Collective salvation means that a person must take care of the group first so they can all be saved before they take care of themselves. For example, it's like the group work assignment in school. All the students in the group get the same grade, although two students really work hard, two students work every now and then and the last two don't work at all. The bottom line is that they all get the same grade. Do you think that is fair? Collective salvation is giving every student in class a "C" to evenly distribute the grades so everybody wins, even though some succeed, some just do enough to get by and others simply fail. The same theory of economics goes with collective salvation. Karl Marx laid the groundwork for collective salvation in *The Communist Manifesto*. His theory was for everybody to receive an equal distribution of the wealth, on the backs of the hard working middle class and rich, whose civic duty would be to pay their fair share. Globally society is moving towards collective salvation and quickly moving away from individual responsibility. Okay, that's enough of the history lesson. What does this have to do with my gram's lesson? Basically, the system is destroying the independence of the individual therefore killing one's self-drive, confidence and esteem. It's no longer up to the individual to achieve their own dreams through blood, sweat and tears. Now they must put all their hard work and dedication into their dreams for the group, not their future. Trust me, this is a very well crafted plan designed to control the people and give power to the few elite.

I watched *Dr. Zhivago* last night and collective salvation really hit home. When the Bolshevik Revolution took over in Russia they just marched into the home of Zhivago's parents and occupied it. The revolutionaries took all of their hard earned possessions and gave them to a bunch of freeloaders because Zhivago and his family needed to share their wealth. I pray that the USA doesn't turn into the United Socialist States of America. Even if it doesn't, collective salvation is already being indoctrinated in our schools. Ladies and gentlemen, you need to be aware of these teachings. Don't stand for it! Don't let someone tell you where you need to give your money and who you need to help. We need to be people of charity as God desires. The government, the church, the politicians and the unions are not God. They have no right to tell you who to give your money to or force you to do so. In reality they want you to give to the freeloaders because it enslaves the poor and guarantees the power stronghold of the elites. Don't be fooled by their lies and the elite telling you that you are helping people out by giving them a handout. How are countries like Greece doing with the handout approach?

Believe in the power you have to achieve your goals and make a positive difference in the lives of others. Believe in the abilities you have been given by God the Father. Believe in the relationship you have with Jesus Christ. He will show you the truth and He will help you accomplish your goals if you talk to Him more than you talk on your IPhony. Believe in yourself and those who love you. Show them you're an Evans, a Smith, an Urban, an individual, a believer in God and an American. Show them you are the best you that you can possibly be. Turn off the incoherent voices in the masses who are telling you that the power of the individual is dead. I truly believe that one person who follows God's way can change the world for the better. George Washington, Martin Luther King Jr., Abraham Lincoln, Rosa Parks – do those names ring a bell? You were born to be great! You were born to lead! You were born to provide light to the many desperate souls trapped in darkness! You were born to make a difference! I believe in you! Believe in the people who believe in you.

Chapter 5: Gram Cibik

PRAYER IS THE MOST POWERFUL THING IN THE WORLD

My Gram Cibik is a peach. She's a cute, little old lady who just brings a smile to your face. She might be the best storyteller I've ever heard. She gets really animated and does a great job giving hand gestures when telling a tale. I always ask her if she wants to come into school as a guest speaker when I teach speaking skills. I think she'd do a great job showing the students how to use body language. She'd probably even bring them in some cookies. Every time I ask her she just says, "Oh, Christopher, stop it." Sure she's a cutie and gives great hand gestures, but that's not why I'm writing about her. My gram believes in the power of prayer. Now I may disagree with her methods of praying, but I cannot disagree with her devout faith in the Lord when it comes to praying. We may have different habits; however there is no question that she gives her prayers directly to the Lord to help those in need. Remember what I told you earlier: That which you gaze upon you will become. Well, I may not have realized it, but seeing my gram pray and her dedication to the Lord sure made an impact on me.

I always believed in God, however my relationship with him was never really number one in my life. I used God out of convenience and I was a deal maker with the Lord. That simply doesn't cut it. I prayed to God when I felt like it, instead of on a daily basis. I would cut deals with God. I'd say, "God, if you introduce me to a great girl I promise that I'll get my act together and stop hanging out in bars." In my early twenties I wasn't much of a Christian or church person. I went to church, but I just did it out of obligation. I was going through a tough time in my life. Someone really showed evil towards me through their actions. I was very bitter and carried a great deal of anger inside of me. This affected my work and relationships with others. Also, at the time I had a buddy who was very ill and in the hospital. I went to go and visit him at the Hershey Medical Center in the evening. I couldn't find his room. I asked at registration and they said he wasn't there. I became a bit worried especially when I could not reach him on the cell phone. The anger boiled up inside of me even more as I recalled the pain of what was done to me. As I walked around the hospital I came across a chapel. Now remember, at this time I wasn't right with the Lord. All of a sudden I just felt this feeling inside moving me to go into the chapel. It was a peaceful and reassuring sensation. I went in. The chapel was beautiful. There was a fountain with flowing waters and fresh plants. To top it off there were kneelers around the flowing waters. It was a while since I prayed to the Lord but I felt the need to get down on my knees and pour out my heart. I did. I asked God to forgive the person for doing me wrong even if he didn't want to repent. I asked the Lord to help me let go and release the chains of bitterness and animosity that were binding me. I let the Lord hear my cries. As I got up from the kneeler and walked away I felt a weight lifted off my shoulders. My walk was no longer as heavy. I felt refreshed and free. I understood the power of prayer.

Get to Work

God desires to have a personal relationship with you through conversation and prayer. He doesn't want you to recite prayers. For example, the only prayer given to us in the Bible is the "Our Father." He wants you to speak from your heart, just like David did, which is evident in psalms. When Jesus prayed to his Father, he revealed his emotions and spoke from his heart. He did not take out a prayer book and start reciting prayers to his Father. If you were to talk to your earthly father would you write down what you wanted to say to him every day and then recite it? Or would you speak from your heart and mind? The same applies with our heavenly father, Jesus Christ. He desires you to pour out your heart. All successful relationships are based on feelings and emotions, not repetitious litanies. To draw closer to people you need to be honest and reveal your inmost feelings. Even if you don't, God will still see what you are trying to hide through tradition.

Sometimes we as humans think we can save ourselves and others during tough times. Don't be foolish because we can't. If we could save ourselves and others then Jesus would not have suffered and died on the cross. We need the power of prayer with our Savior Jesus Christ to clean our house or clean up our life. We need the Lord to tie our shoes and tie the knot of love and honor of our marriage. The bottom line is that we need the Lord for everything, every single day. We can't help everybody. We need to take the burden off our backs and give our struggles up to the Lord. That's why he suffered and died on the cross for us. We shouldn't feel guilty about not being able to solve problems or heal the wounds of ourselves and others on our own. Like any great friend, the best thing we can say to the Lord is, "God, I need your help. Please show me the way." Don't you, as a great friend, get excited when someone asks you for help? In response you'd put on your work boots and get going to help your friend. The Lord does the same. But when we go to the Lord with our prayers, there's just a little difference: His help is divine, miraculous and supernatural. If you truly believe in the love of our Lord and Savior Jesus Christ, then you will understand how prayer is the most powerful thing in the world.

Chapter 6: Uncle Andy
DO THINGS YOUR WAY

Frank Sinatra sang, "For what is a man, what has he got/If not himself then he has not/To say the things he truly feels/And not the words of one who kneels/The record shows I took the blows/ And did it my way/Yes it was my way." I can't think of a song that defines my Uncle Andy better than "My Way," sung by Frank Sinatra. Between the ages of 18 and 20 I was going to college and enjoying life. Between the ages of 18 and 20 my Uncle Andy was fighting the Germans. My uncle was a survivor of D-Day. He was injured in the battle and never shied away from showing his love for America—that he learned to appreciate much more after his World War II experience. After the war my uncle owned and operated a floral shop and was very active with his fellow soldiers through veteran associations. Uncle Andy was also responsible for starting the first Little League in his community. After my grandfather died my Uncle Andy really stepped up to the plate and took on the role of my gramp. He always used to pick me up after school and bring me Kit Kat candy bars. My uncle was always there for me. He never missed an event I was a part of, be it sports or school. I certainly remember my Uncle Andy as a proud veteran who really did everything for his nephew, but what I learned the most from him was how to do things your way.

I loved my Uncle Andy, however if anyone could really aggravate you, it was him. I think my uncle probably had more enemies in life than friends. The reason for his conflicts was because there was only one way to do things with Uncle Andy, his way. I was grateful that my uncle gave me side jobs like cutting his grass, painting and cleaning. He paid me more than I deserved, but let me tell you, it was no treat. The work wasn't tough at all. Uncle Andy was. He watched me like a hawk and would constantly be barking orders at me. I remember one time when he was out in the yard with his cane and yelling at me to cut this certain part of the lawn. I said, "Uncle Andy, there's only small stones there. There's no grass." It didn't matter to him. If he said he wanted it cut, he wanted it cut. So I cut the stones with the lawnmower. Cars were driving by and you could hear the little pebbles dinging off the vehicles. When I moved to the beach my senior year in college my father took on the chores for my uncle. When I came back my dad said, "I don't know how the heck you worked for him. He was a pain in the neck." Come hell or high water, it was Uncle Andy's way or the highway.

Get to Work

This is going to be a tough one to give you some motivation. Do I want you to be stubborn? No. Do I want you to conflict with people? No. Do I want you to be tough to work for? No. So, then what is it that Uncle Andy is trying to tell us. I think Uncle Andy would want me to tell you to have confidence in what you do and when you know what you're doing, don't let anybody tell you to do it in a way that is not best for you. Basically, don't let people compromise your integrity. So, I'm sure you'll be called miserable, bossy and stubborn. That's okay. What's right is right and what's wrong is wrong. The 10 commandments given by our Lord prove that those things will never change. So why should you have to change your interpretations of God's law? You don't, so don't. Reggie White was a Hall of Fame football player and also a devout Christian. His nickname was "The Minister of Defense." He made public prayer between opposing players, who were trying to kill each other, prevalent after games. He also made his views about homosexuality and its destruction of the family very public. He gave a speech on the topic in Madison, Wisconsin in front of legislatures. He really caused great conflict after that with players, the media and gay groups. He spoke God's teaching to the people and didn't back down. Like Uncle Andy, he did things his way. Sure, he could have kept his beliefs to himself, but he was so confident in what was right and wrong that he vetted them in a public forum. Like Uncle Andy, he wasn't afraid to stand up even if he made enemies with many people. Uncle Andy was really good at arguing with people. My gram always knew when to get dinner ready because she'd be able to hear him and the neighbor arguing about Ross Perot when he was running for president. **ADD Moment: By the way, Uncle Andy loved Ross Perot and wasn't too crazy about Bill Clinton.** In the end, I will always have the upmost respect for Uncle Andy for doing things his way although he really pressed my buttons at times and made me cut stones instead of grass. I'm just thankful one of those pebbles didn't go through a car's windshield. Here's the secret: If you are right with the Lord through a personal relationship and Scripture, you may think you're doing things your way, but you'll be doing things His way. Get one with the Lord, do things your way and you'll be honoring His way.

Chapter 7: Uncle Franky

WHEN YOU RUSH, ACCIDENTS HAPPEN

95. That's how old my great-great-Uncle Franky is. He's the self-proclaimed patriarch of the family. Uncle Franky lived during the Great Depression where he worked in the CC camps. He's seen it all: World War II, the birth of rock and roll, the Korean War, the Kennedy Assassination, the Vietnam War, the Civil Rights Movement, the alternative lifestyle trend, and the continued destruction of our nation and the family unit. Through it all, he's always watched EWTN, although most of the time he's sleeping. As he continues to age and call 911 by accident, he gives off his wisdom. **ADD Moment: He accidentally called 911 twice and the police came to the house because they thought something happened. On the phone you have to dial a 9, then 1, then the area code before calling long distance. He thought he forgot to dial the 1, so he hit it again. The result: Police came to the house**

because he called 911. His wisdom is precious. When relatives call him on the phone and ask him how he's doing he says, "I'm at the mercy of the Big Boss." That's wisdom. We are all at the mercy of our heavenly Father.

Uncle Frank worked at Pennsylvania Power and Electric for 58 years. He was a solider during World War II, stationed in Hawaii. He's the only known solider to be injured when a coconut hit him in the head. Through the years Uncle Franky would always tell us stories that revealed his wisdom. I remember him telling me about his brother, Jimmy, who played football and died young due to all the pounding his body took. At the time I was in my early 20s and playing in a very competitive flag football league which was more like tackle. I remember my uncle telling me over Thanksgiving break that I'd better stop playing unless I wanted to be crippled for life. One week later I broke my nose and tore my right ACL during a game. How's that for wisdom? The one phrase my uncle always repeats is: When you rush, accidents happen. I learned that lesson the hard way.

I was a very busy person with teaching, coaching, officiating basketball and umpiring baseball, graduate school, training and competing. There were times when I went to bed at midnight and got up at 4 AM to workout. Sometimes I would ride the bike at the gym with my eyes closed. That type of lifestyle fosters rushing. Well, a few years ago rushing almost cost me my life. I came home from school and I had to eat really quickly so I could go to my internship.

I needed to eat because I had to go to the gym after the internship. I needed to eat immediately because if I ate before I worked out, then I'd be bloated. I was eating beef and watching the highlights on Sportscenter when I developed this horrible heartburn. I've had this before and it usually went away. This time it didn't. I couldn't swallow. I kept on spitting and every time I swallowed I felt my saliva go a ways down and then rebound and come right back up. I would get major coughing spells where I'd be doubled over. I didn't want to call 911 because I didn't want to see an ambulance pick me up. None of my family was home. I didn't know if I'd be able to make it up the road to the Urgent Care Center. I had to make a move for medical assistance before I choked to death. I got in my truck and took off. As I turned onto the highway I started choking again on my saliva. Normally there were cars parked all along the side of the road. Thank God because that day there happened to be on open spot right as I made the turn. If that spot wasn't there I probably would have been in a major accident and who knows what the result would have been. Thankfully I made it to Urgent Care and they were able to reach my Aunt Katie who took me to the hospital for an emergency endoscopy. I had to have another one a month later so they could enlarge my esophagus. I spent many years rushing and eating very quickly. I ate well but I ate quickly and late at night which caused my esophagus to shrink. That was why I choked. If I would have always listened to Uncle Franky's wisdom then I would not have had the most expensive piece of beef in the world.

Get to Work

The world went and got itself in one big hurry. We have fast food, fast cars, high speed internet, twenty-minute abs and so on. We've taken every task and invention and put iton the Autobahn. In certain religions they even have fast services. I've got one thing to say about all the speed in our society: Easy Big Fella! Have you ever tried to drive in an inner city? Everyone is in a big rush to get to the same place. Drivers have no idea how to merge. Everyone is a bundle of nerves. I rarely see drivers waving another car on. I see many middle fingers and other inappropriate gestures, but very few nice, friendly waves. It's a downright disaster and the perfect example of how rushing causes accidents.

Our society has grown accustomed to being busy. It's become a necessity. We always have to be busy doing something. We feel attached and connected to the things we do. Busyness gives us a sense of accomplishment. It enhances our egos. Without busyness we feel empty. We have to work, go to graduate school, coach little league, take a Zumba class, and volunteer to teach bible school. And we have to do all of these things at once. Do you think someone who's involved in all of these things actually does a good job? They might be mediocre but they will never achieve excellence. You are much better off doing a few things really well then doing many things with mediocrity. Jesus was not a mediocre man and he does not expect us to be just average in what we do. He focused on his ministry and spreading the Good News. He didn't worry about cooking, cleaning, exercising, and other things. If He focused on being busy then He would not have perfected his work. Instead, He kept his agenda simple and achieved excellence. The example He left behind for us is still saving sinners and spreading Christianity. We continue His work through the example He set.

When you try to do many things, you rush and then accidents happen. The more we involve ourselves with worldly tasks the further we drift away from the Lord. The biggest accident we could make is putting our relationship with Jesus Christ on the backburner. We'll be successful at doing that if we involve ourselves with many things. How can God speak to you if you're always busy? He can't. Slow down and focus on the talents God has given you. Make your talents the things you do. That is certainly honoring God. Focus on getting busy with the Lord through prayer and Scripture. Get involved in healthy fellowship and find a ministry that won't spread you thin. Spend your time eating dinner and watching a movie with the family. Push all the unworthy tasks to the side forever. If you don't then I can guarantee you that you will rush and accidents will happen.

Chapter 8: Joe Grella

"GET THE ROOTS!"

The few, the proud, the St. Al's boys. This was the motto my first boss, Joe Grella, would always proclaim. We were few and proud and we did work at St. Aloysius church, rectory, and school. How were we few? Well, there weren't many high school and college kids willing to clean toilets, empty garbage, cut grass, mop and wax floors, pull weeds, stack chairs, shovel snow, paint and so much more during the summer time and on days off during the school year. We did it all and earned $3 an hour when most young men were sleeping in or playing video games. I will always look back on those days with very fond memories. Joe Grella played a huge part in shaping me into the man that I am today. Unfortunately, when I was 14 I thought he was my worst enemy. Here's why.

Joe Grella recruited me to work at St. Al's when I was 14 years old. He knew I was athletic and a decent kid. I didn't realize back then that his goal was to mold me into a man. So, somewhat against my parents' wishes, who just wanted me to focus on sports, I decided to start working. That was my way of honoring my mom and dad; putting on my work boots and going to work. I had a ton of fun with Joe, but there were also many times in which he really got under my skin. Everything I did just didn't seem good enough for Joe. At times he would really get on me. Sometimes the pressure was really intense and you just wanted to walk out on him. Sometimes I did. Thank God for Vince Williamson because he always brought me back. Weeding the shrub beds was one of the jobs that I didn't do too well. Joe would come and inspect my work and he'd start yelling, "Get the roots! Get the roots!" Most times he'd come to inspect my work and he'd find roots. I swear I think he planted roots in certain spots just to show me I didn't do a good enough job. It was tough to satisfy Joe. Although it was tough at times to show up for work, deep down inside I knew that he really cared about me. He'd break you down to the point where you couldn't be broken anymore. But in the end he showed just enough affection to build you back up and make you want to work for him. Joe told me to "Get the roots!" countless times, however it had nothing to do with getting the roots. It had everything to do with doing everything the right way, even those things you didn't like to do.

Get to Work

Young boys need more men like Joe Grella in their lives. We need that tough love in order to become the natural leaders God created us to become. Every job I had after working two years with Joe was a piece of cake. Landscaping, warehouse work, construction, garbage collecting, security, counseling, teaching and coaching are all demanding jobs. I had to work hard, but I was mentally prepared for any task my boss had placed before me. I was mentally prepared to work harder than anybody else and do anything the boss asked me to do. When on the grounds crew at the Wyoming Valley Country Club, I had to wear a complete rain suit and weedwack in 90 degree heat all day long in an area that had poison ivy and sumac. I did it like it was nothing. Joe prepared me for that moment and so many more. When things are going haywire at school, I feel the pressure and step up to the plate. The pressure gets me fired up to solve the problem in the midst of chaos and to provide a positive atmosphere.

Joe was a mastermind; he knew exactly what he was doing when he would get on me and yell, "Get the roots!" If you could find a Joe Grella in your life, be grateful. I know you'll hate him at times, but the impact he will have on your future will be profound. If you don't have a Joe Grella in your life then try to find one. They're out there. If you can't, find a job that is dirty and do it to the best of your ability. I teach and I used to coach every day. I appreciate that so much, knowing that it all started with pulling weeds in hot summer weather for $3 an hour when my friends were swimming in the pool and eating ice cream. On my first day of substitute teaching, December 15, 2003, I was paid with a $60 check as I walked out the door. The first thought that came to my mind was, "I can't believe

I'm actually getting paid for substituting for an absent teacher." It was and still is an awesome feeling to get paid for doing what I love to do and what God has planned for me to do. You will enjoy and succeed at everything you do in life if, at first, you learn to "Getthe roots!"

Chapter 9: Coach Jim Stone
WORKING TO WIN IS EVERYTHING

God blessed me with athletic abilities. My father always used to tell me that I was a natural. Sports just came easy to me. When I was on the court or the field, I was in my realm. My fondest memories of competing come from youth sports. The greatest coaches I had were those who coached Little League baseball. They volunteered and did it because they wanted to teach us the principles of teamwork, fundamentals and winning. I know this might sound like a shock for youngsters nowadays, but I played Little League at a time when you didn't receive a trophy for just showing up. Competition was our creed. There wasn't a bigger competitor than Coach Jim Stone. There also wasn't a coach who was more criticized than him. He looked and acted like a platoon leader. He walked with a firm, quick step, wore his hat close to the forehead and pointed downward and styled a crew cut and handlebar mustache like Hulk Hogan. He looked like a real man. I was blessed to be selected as an all star when I was twelve and given the opportunity to be coached by Jim Stone. It was an honor to play for Coach Jim Stone. I would have run through hell with a can of gasoline for that man. Here's why.

The biggest dream for a Little League baseball player is to compete in the Little League World Series in Williamsport, Pennsylvania. Our all star teams dominated opponents prior to playing on the District 16 team. If we won enough tournaments we could potentially play in Williamsport. I really believed that we had the players capable of making a run for Williamsport. When we played together in the past as a team we were very successful. Now we had a few new players added to the arsenal and a coach who was feared, revered and had the reputation of being a drill sergeant, demanding excellence from his troops. Parents really didn't care for him. They said he was too tough on kids. They said he was a "win-at-all-cost coach." I kind of liked the negative attention he ignited. I remember watching all star games when I was younger. I was in admiration of the passion and intensity of Coach Stone. I remember one time when a player hit a home run to win the game and Coach Stone embraced him at home plate with a huge bear hug. No matter what the outsiders said, I knew there was something special about Coach Stone. When I heard I was going to play for him, I was ready to go to work.

Coach Stone coached with no strings attached; he had no kids playing in the league like many other coaches. We were his children. In the summer of 1993 I learned what focus, dedication and discipline was all about. Our all star practices were all about fundamentals. If you didn't catch a baseball with two hands, then you had to learn in order to play for Coach Stone. We had two practice sessions during the summer of 1993. In the morning at 8 AM we would work on the fundamentals of fielding, base running and pitching. For two hours we didn't even pick up a baseball bat. We would get a 10 to 15 minute break in the morning session. During this time Coach Stone and his assistant would go to the concession stand to grade us. I remember Coach Stone would always say, "Keep it down to a mild roar," before he went to assess our skills. It was all business, all the time with him. We would then go home for lunch and spend the afternoon resting. Coach Stone did not permit anyone to go swimming. Sure, it sounds like a harsh decree to tell young boys that they couldn't go for a swim on a hot summer day. However, he knew that if we swam we would be exhausted for batting practice in the early evening. Batting practice was rapid fire. You just had to hit and hit and hit. If your fundamentals were out of synch you would receive individual instruction. The individual was never mentioned in our dugout. Coach Stone stressed the importance of teamwork. If any player lacked discipline, sportsmanship and teamwork Coach Stone would not tolerate it. If you broke the team covenant you had to run and run and run. We were talented enough to win and through all of our training we were built to win. Most importantly we were playing for a coach who was supposedly a win-at-all-cost guy. We had all the ingredients needed to achieve victory and please our demanding coach. It was time to play ball.

What was the result of this winning combination? We lost well before the fans, the players and our coach expected us to. We had some success but we certainly underachieved. Our season came to an end against Harvey's Lake. The loss eliminated us from the District 16 tournament. As we sat in the dugout after the game I can recall how devastated I felt. I was crushed. After winning so many championships in years past, we let the biggest one slip through our fingers. We would not be moving on to other tournaments with the potential of playing in the Little League World Series. Most of all I was crushed because I felt like I let Coach Stone down. This was a man who gave his all for us. He didn't take off work to relax at the beach and drink pina coladas. He used his vacation days to teach young boys the game of baseball during a crucial time in their lives. I just wanted to hoist that championship trophy for him because I knew that he truly cared about us and he certainly gave us every ounce of energy he had in the tank. He truly deserved a championship and I felt like a complete failure because we didn't win one for him. With all these emotions running wild I just couldn't contain myself anymore. Right there in the dugout I broke down in tears. What happened next was one of the greatest moments of my life.

Coach Stone came over to me, grabbed me by the shoulders, pulled me into his chest and wrapped his arms around me. The tears were coming out like a waterfall and I kept on saying, "I'm sorry. I'm sorry." After hearing these words Coach Stone pulled me in even tighter and he rubbed my back. In response to my apology and weeping Coach Stone said, "It's okay son. It's okay son. I'm very proud of you. Everything is going to be all right." I can still feel the warm embrace of Coach Stone twenty-one years later. Those parents and players who never gave Jim Stone a chance by opening up their minds and hearts to him will never see the man I loved and looked up to as a role model in the summer of 1993. It's been twenty-one years since I've seen Coach Stone. I sometimes wonder what he might be doing now. Sadly, he probably isn't coaching anymore. Parents tried to run him out of town twenty years ago. I could only imagine what the soft and entitled crop of parents would do to him nowadays. Although Coach Stone has been physically missing from my life since I was in 6th grade, I still feel his presence and impact more now as a thirty-two year old man than I ever did. I thank God for blessing me to play for Coach Stone. He did not win a championship on the field. He did win a championship in the lives of those who observed and listened.

Get to Work

Do you want to achieve excellence? If you answered "yes" to this question then we're on the same page. If you answered "yes" then you must understand that there is a price to pay. Excellence doesn't come easy or in a worldly package labeled "instant gratification." If you believe the ads on television and the infomercials on how to make millions of dollars then I have some advice: Wake up! The price you will have to pay to earn excellence comes in one simple four letter word that is too often forgotten: Work. Sorry, but this does not mean you earn a passing grade just by showing up for class. Work involves the grind, the sweat, the blood and the tears. You don't work hard every now and then. You work hard all the time, no matter what you do. Jesus didn't preach the message of his Father when he felt like it. He spoke the word of God all the time. Talent and status are all hype. Hard work is everlasting. Jesus wasn't a man who rode the wave of fame for a short period of time. Remember, Jesus wasn't concerned about his status. He was a feather ruffling kind of a guy who was eventually tortured and crucified because he didn't fit the status quo of the high priests and Pharisees. Coach Jim Stone too was a worker like Jesus who carried a thick skin with him. He coached the only way he knew how to: hard and with the favor of truth on his side. It wasn't easy for both Jesus and Coach Stone and it won't be easy for you.

Although it won't be easy, it sure will be worth it. Hard work is the first price you will have to pay. The second sacrifice will be to associate yourself with great peers and great teachers. George Washington said that "he'd rather be alone than in bad company." If the peers you hang around with are bad company then give them a good old "Adios!" In order to achieve excellence you need to be around peers who are going to lift you up instead of bring you down. Drinking, gambling, using foul language, being lazy and acting irresponsibly are not hobbies and traits that will bring out the best in you. Jesus tried to help people with these problems; however, his core group of friends was the apostles. They were mere sinners who believed in the Lord and were trying their best to live righteous lives. If you want to achieve excellence in your life then I highly recommend that you ditch the weekend friends and find a solid group of believers like Jesus did. Secondly, I urge you to learn from mentors who are hard-nosed and still loving like Coach Stone. If you're screwing up, a great teacher will let you know about it and won't be afraid to punish you. Tough love is needed unless you want to be coddled the rest of your life. Your pursuit of excellence will not be a part time job. It's a 24/7 honor that never allows you to take your hands off the wheel. The result will be insults. The result will be worldly failures. So be it. The only result that matters is earning the favor of the Lord Jesus Christ because he knows that working to win is everything.

Chapter 10: Mr. Litchkofski

DON'T EVER CHANGE

Did you ever have a person come into your life who just made an explosion? When I say explosion I mean it in a good way. When I was in 6th grade I had a substitute teacher who hit me like a ton of bricks. I observed him and for the first time I saw the type of man I hoped to become someday. He was smart, passionate, energetic, funny and thoughtful. I looked at Mr. James Litchkofski as a twelve-year-old and I said, "That's it! He's got it. He's the real deal. He has what I want to find within myself." God blessed me to have Mr. Litchkofski as a substitute teacher for the next two years. God connected me to Mr. L. and we are still close to this day. You know what's amazing? He was just a substitute teacher and he made a life changing impact on me.

As a young man I was just trying to find myself and my place in the world. Who was Christopher Michael Kasian? What was he going to do with his life? The truth is, I had no idea. I knew I wanted to make an impact and do something great. I wanted to explode into the lives of people like Mr. L. did for me. Well, you know the story that's common with so many young adults. I got in the way of God's purpose for my life. The world got in the way of God's purpose for my life. I got older and hung around with people I should have avoided and did things I should not have done. The whole while, I was desperately searching the world trying to find meaning within my very heart and soul. The world left me feeling completely empty like a broken down pickup on the side of a lonely desert highway. Through the blessing of God, some people saw meaning in the life of a disillusioned young man. The catalyst was James Litchkofski, my elementary substitute teacher.

During my years with Mr. L. as a teacher he would always ask me, "What happened to you, Kasian? You don't know, do you?" My selfdescription in our 8th grade yearbook was "different." Sure, I may not have known who I was but I was certain of the fact that I was unlike the other kids. I thought differently, acted differently and dreamed differently. I was just a bit lost in the world, and sometimes I guess I curiously wondered what really did happen. Why was I the only one to seem really bothered when kids got picked on? Why was I the only one who wanted a girlfriend just to treat her right? Why was I the only one who felt the need to sit in the back of the church and just talk to God? There were many more "whys" I was asking myself, so you could understand the wondering if something really did happen to me. Now, let me explain to you that Mr. L. asked me that question in a comical way and not with the intent to make me feel strange or to embarrass me. I didn't feel strange. I just knew that I was on a journey that may have been different from most of the kids. I felt something deep within my heart but I just didn't know if it was for real.

After 8th grade you graduate from St. Aloysius and are off to high school. Although we had small classes of twenty to twenty-five students, the 8th grade graduation is usually a big deal. When you graduate from St. Aloysius you are given a yearbook. It's a tradition that students and teachers sign it and write you a personal note as you head into the big, bad world of high school. The note that changed my life and that I would always return to on my journey was the one Mr. L. left me. He wrote: "Chris, the best advice I can give you is to never change. You're great just the way you are." Wow! Talk about a powerful statement of faith in a young man's life. Words do change the world and they do change a life. As I went through my struggles with faith, relationships and growing pains, I always returned to the words of Mr. L. I'm the man I am today because the one person who connected with me and who I looked up to as a role model showed a belief in who I was and what I was capable of becoming. Who would have thought that it would have come from a substitute teacher? God certainly works in mysterious ways.

Get to Work

Mr. L. saw right through to the core of me. He saw the man I was capable of becoming even though I disguised who I was with worldly things as I was growing up. Be grateful for the people in your life who see the inner beauty that you've been trying to hide. Listen to them. Believe them. If God hasn't blessed you with a person who has great faith in you, there's no need to panic. Your situation can be completely dire. Maybe you have bad parents or go to a bad school and have no friends. Maybe you're an orphan. Don't worry! Earthly people do not need to see your inner beauty. In the Old Testament Joseph's own brothers failed to see any beauty in him and out of jealousy they plotted evil plans against him. In the New Testament the apostle Peter, who said he loved Jesus, allowed temptation to get in the way and denied Him three times. Jesus was left alone to hang on the cross, but he knew there was his Almighty Father who saw His son's inner beauty. Jesus used his faith in the Lord to forgive those who did him wrong. Do you remember the words He spoke while hanging on the cross? "Father, forgive them for they know not what they do." What does this mean?

I was going through a time when I was being criticized and misunderstood by my family for walking closer with the Lord. They were upset that I finally saw the light and heard the gospel and made the decision to leave the Catholic Church. My family thought I was crazy for quoting Scripture and praising Jesus and America's founding values. I am crazy. I'm crazy about Jesus and I'm crazy about America. I was a bit disappointed because the people I expected to have faith in me were losing their belief in the man I was becoming. I went for a walk that day with these thoughts on my mind. I noticed something carved in the gravel. Guess what it said? "Jesus loves you." To the person reading these very lines right now: Jesus loves you too! He sees right through the mask of bitterness or sadness that you've put on. He sees right through the mask of phoniness that you've draped yourself in. He sees right through the mask of the worldly person you've allowed yourself to become. He sees your heart, your soul, your mind and the inner beauty that they share. He sees the person He has created you to be, not the person you've allowed yourself to become. He sees a diamond in the rough. Maybe you've gotten off track. Maybe you think you're on track but you really haven't dug deep enough inside of yourself. Now's the time to do so. Trust the Lord! When you open up your heart to Jesus Christ and allow Him to see your inner beauty you'll begin to realize that you won't ever have to change.

Chapter 11: Sister Andrea

"INTEGRITY IS TO..."

...Know what is right, do what is right and not be ashamed of doing what is right." Those were the words of Sister Andrea, who was my high school English and German teacher. When we would misbehave as a class she'd repeat the integrity maxim over and over. Sister Andrea was a tough, no nonsense teacher. She was a disciplinarian and a conservative. You did not want to get on her bad side. She had a look that would pierce your heart. She expected you to do the right thing, all the time. There was no positive reinforcement for doing the right thing. Being attentive, showing respect and working hard earned you a good grade. That was Sister Andrea's method for a positive awards system. She was old school. The old fashioned way is the only school she knew was capable of teaching young adults the lessons needed to become men and women of integrity.

I know this might sound like a surprise to modern public school teachers and students, but there was no such thing as Attention Deficit

Disorder, Attention Deficit Hyperactivity Disorder or Oppositional Defiance Disorder in Sister Andrea's class. Your responsibility as a student was to listen and obey the one classroom rule: integrity. If you misbehaved, Sister Andrea would scold you. If you were not paying attention and didn't know an answer to a question, then Sister would wait, sometimes the entire period, until you found the correct answer. I'll never forget during Freshman English class when she asked a student a question and he didn't know the answer. This was an answer he should have known if he was paying attention. Unfortunately, to his demise he was not listening and failed to give the correct answer. Sister refused to move on with the lesson. Instead, she waited the entire class period until he discovered the correct answer. To the student's dismay the others in class were laughing at him. That didn't bother Sister Andrea because she knew he brought the mockery on himself by not listening. I don't recall if he ever came up with the correct answer. I do recall that no matter what, in Sister Andrea's class you were to listen. There was also no such thing as depression or personality and behavior disorders in Sister Andrea's class. No matter how bad your circumstances, you appreciated the life God gave you and the opportunity you had to rise above any hardships. Most importantly, you always treated people the way you wanted to be treated, even if you weren't treated well. You may be wondering how Sister got her students to perform. She must've had some magic teaching style that engaged students. Before you get excited, let me tell you something: there were no fireworks in Sister's Andrea's teaching methods. She just kept it simple and it worked for me.

In Sister Andrea's class there was no cooperative learning, differentiated instruction or technology integration. This also would be a shock for current public school teachers and students. Sister Andrea used lecture and chalk, that's it. Believe it or not, we were actually taught grammar and vocabulary in high school. We even diagrammed sentences. There's a poster I usually put up in my classroom that has the words of Garfield. It simply says, "You are responsible for you." Sister Andrea set up her classroom in a way that would have pleased our Founding Fathers. In order to succeed in her class you needed to be self reliant. It didn't matter if you worked alone or in a group. It didn't matter if the teacher gave a lecture or had a classroom discussion. It didn't matter if the teacher used chalk and a blackboard or an overhead projector. The only thing that mattered was your ability to rely completely on yourself to be successful. Like I stated earlier, Sister was very conservative. She always re-used paper for tests, quizzes and notes. You did not want to throw away any piece of paper that still had one good side left. She would find a way to reuse the paper in the future. Sister was truly a woman of integrity. She didn't get caught up in educational trends. She based her classroom environment on God's laws rather than societal contrived bureaucracies. She may not have won a popularity contest amongst both teachers and students, but to Sister Andrea hype didn't matter. She wasn't ashamed of doing what was right in the eyes of the Lord.

Get to Work

The innermost part of our hearts, minds and souls knows what is right. We know the path of integrity because the good Lord already paved the way. The road to righteousness is narrow and not easy to travel. God didn't say it would be easy, but He knew it would be worth it. Sadly, the world tells us to take the easy way out. A life of integrity is too hard and stressful. Take the wide open road, follow many others and be free. These are the maxims the 21st century Breakdown Society. These are the maxims of Generation Me. These are harsh realities but there's another one that's even more destructive. Do you know what's worse than this? Sin is rewarded. It's bad enough that sinful nature is real and looked at indifferently in our culture. It's downright sickening to realize that sinful people are given championship rings for their evil behavior. All of this is occurring on the TV screens and the internet while young children in broken homes observe and learn what is good through the deceptive eyes of the prince of darkness.

If you've gotten off track and need a refresher course, then let's get to work. If you're completely lost then now is the time for the truth that lies within your very heart, mind and soul to be found. Let me remind you that we are still sinners. Only Jesus was perfect and free of sin. We will stumble. When we fall the Lord will always pick us up if we believe in Him and try our best to fulfill His commandments. So, if you've forgotten, here's your refresher course:

The Ten Commandments

¹ And God spoke all these words:

² "I am the LORD your God, who brought you out of Egypt, out of the land of slavery.

³ "You shall have no other gods before me.

⁴ "You shall not make for yourself an image in the form of anything in heaven above or on the earth beneath or in the waters below. ⁵ You shall not bow down to them or worship them; for I, the LORD your God, am a jealous God, punishing the children for the sin of the parents to the third and fourth generation of those who hate me, ⁶ but showing love to a thousand generations of those who love me and keep my commandments.

⁷ "You shall not misuse the name of the LORD your God, for the LORD will not hold anyone guiltless who misuses his name.

⁸ "Remember the Sabbath day by keeping it holy. ⁹ Six days you shall labor and do all your work, ¹⁰ but the seventh day is a Sabbath to the LORD your God. On it you shall not do any work, neither you, nor your son or daughter, nor your male or female servant, nor your animals, nor any foreigner residing in your towns. ¹¹ For in six days the LORD made the heavens and the earth, the sea, and all that is in them, but he rested on the seventh day. Therefore the LORD blessed the Sabbath day and made it holy.

¹² "Honor your father and your mother, so that you may live long in the land the LORD your God is giving you.

[13] "You shall not murder.

[14] "You shall not commit adultery.

[15] "You shall not steal.

[16] "You shall not give false testimony against your neighbor.

[17] "You shall not covet your neighbor's house. You shall not covet your neighbor's wife, or his male or female servant, his ox or donkey, or anything that belongs to your neighbor."

Following the Ten Commandments and repenting and turning our hearts back to the Lord when we fall truly defines integrity and the example displayed through Sister Andrea. Once you give your life to the Lord He will work through you to develop your character so you can live with integrity by knowing what is right, doing what is right and never being ashamed of doing what is right.

Chapter 12: Coach Teddy Napierkowksi

BE GRATEFUL FOR WHAT YOU HAVE, NOT UNGRATEFUL FOR WHAT YOU DON'T

Teddy was the gentlest man I ever met. He talked and moved so softly. I never heard him raise his voice, not even once. That was no easy task for someone who worked with young boys with hormones and mischievous minds ready to rock and roll. He had such a calm way about him. His demeanor was contagious. When around him everybody toned their noise down. He was the conductor of serenity. **ADD Moment: We could certainly use some of that nowadays.** He was extremely humble and grateful for the life he had. I never once heard him boast or even hint at talking about himself. Teddy never talked about Teddy. The topics of his conversations were those he cared about. And they were the young boys that he coached in baseball and helped become umpires. I never met a person so grateful who probably had every reason to be ungrateful.

Teddy Napierkowski was born without any arms. From the get-go God created Teddy with major disabilities. He was certainly behind the eight ball and up against it. They tried experiments on Teddy to provide him with artificial but useable limbs. He gave it a try and eventually he chose to be who he was, a man born without arms. He chose not to alter God's beautiful creation even though the world may have looked at him differently. He was an avid sports fan who would never have the opportunity to play ball. He couldn't wash himself, brush his teeth, prepare his food, change his clothes or even go to the bathroom by himself. And never once did I hear Teddy complain. He easily could have cursed God for not making him like the other boys and girls. Teddy didn't. He easily could have sat around the house and watched television. Teddy didn't. Instead, Teddy turned his disabilities into abilities. Life gave him lemons and he made some lemonade. Instead of sulking Teddy used his abilities to help hundreds of young boys. Teddy became a baseball coach, which he did for many years. He knew the game extremely well. He instructed with his wisdom and his heart, not his hands or arms. He kept the book for the games by writing with his toes. Like I said earlier, you just had to be in Teddy's presence for his life to have an impact on you. How often do you see a baseball coach with no arms who keeps the scorebook with his toes? Teddy was also an umpire and an umpire teacher. Yes, you heard it right; a man with no arms was a Little League umpire. Let me tell you that Teddy was one of the best umpires I ever saw. I have fond memories of helping him place his mask and chest guard on between innings. He even used his talents to help high school kids become Little League umpires. Reflecting back on Teddy just amazes me. I remember him showing up for games in his flannel shirt. He'd have his bag of necessary supplies hanging around his neck. He'd always be wearing a smile and eager for a conversation. As I look back I realized that I was in the presence of a man who was truly touched by God and God was using him to impact the lives of others. Many times I would drive Teddy home from practice or a game. We never once talked about faith or the Lord. We didn't need to. I always saw and felt a light inside of a man who easily could have given his life to darkness. I felt Teddy's humility, warmth, kindness and compassion. He truly cared about people. Teddy loved the life the Lord gave him and how he lived it was a true "thank you" letter to Jesus Christ. I haven't seen Teddy since I was 16 years old. Since then he's passed on. All I can say is that I have a picture of him hanging on my classroom wall. Anytime a student complains about school I tell them about Teddy and I show them his picture.

Get to Work

We're living in a nation whereby the glass of water for many people is half empty. For some people it's not just half empty; their glass is spilled and broken. Why? I guess it's because we have it too good in America. We're so used to having things handed to us and being dependent on our government that we don't know what to do when we have to get down on our knees, get a little dirty and earn a living. A great wakeup call would be for the entire nation to take a weeklong trip to a Communist country like China or a Sharia Law-dominated society like Iran. If seeing Christians persecuted, woman demeaned, children starving, masses of people worshipping dictators and freedom destroyed doesn't wake people up, then I don't know what will. I would pray that such a field trip would help people start to realize how good we have it in the USA.

Here's the bottom line: God has blessed all of us simply by creating us, no matter how we came to form or what circumstances we were born into. What matters most is that we are all created in God's image and likeness and that we truly are God's greatest creation. Maybe you're not happy. Maybe your parents are divorced. Maybe you don't know your father. Maybe you have physical, mental or emotional limitations. Maybe you've had to live a very hard life. So, why even waste negative energy focusing on the bad things? Let's instead focus on the most positive aspect of your life: no matter who you are or how bad you've been, Jesus loves you. He loves you so much that He saw your face thousands of years ago when he was hanging on that cross on Calvary Hill. He gave His life for you. Once you accept Jesus Christ into your life as your Lord and Savior He will give you the gift of the Holy Spirit that will shine a light inside of you. He will make you new again and continually bless you. The light the Lord will give you will be a beacon for others trapped in darkness. You will be a new creation, a person like Teddy Napierkowski, who will look to the Lord and be grateful for what you have and not ungrateful for what you have not.

Chapter 13: Ed Ackerman

THE GREATEST THING YOU CAN GIVE SOMEONE IS YOUR TIME

"Just call me Ed" was my college speech professor's first instruction to his pupils. I was blessed to have Ed Ackerman as my college speech professor during my sophomore year of college. There was only one other instruction that he gave during speech class, "Be yourself." Ed's syllabus was the meaning of life. His rubric for speaking was to pour out your heart. College professors are often stereotyped as self-proclaimed intellectual elites that make big paychecks, work few hours and carry a pompous demeanor and a socialist ideology. Not Ed. He was just your ordinary, average guy who spent many extra hours helping students, acted with humility and was conservative. Let's just say that he was way out of place for academia. He may have been out of place but I was grateful to find my place in his class.

The Greatest Thing You Can Give Someone Is Your Time

Did you ever notice how God always puts people in your life at just the right time? If you're in need of a friend, He will provide it. If you're in need of advice, He will give you a person of wisdom. When I was nineteen or twenty, I really needed someone to listen to me. Ed was the guy. He wasn't just a great speech professor who taught many valuable lessons; he was a friend and a mentor. I always kept my feelings bottled up on the inside. I just never felt comfortable sharing my feelings with my parents. Well, I was at a turning point in my life when I really needed someone. I didn't really have a relationship with the Lord, but he still blessed me with a man who would listen to my heart like Ed.

I spent countless number of hours in Ed's office during his free time telling him about my life and problems. Ed taught me that the greatest thing you can give someone is your time. He gave plenty of that to a young man who was just trying to find his place in the world. Ed never turned me down. He'd buy me lunch and we'd talk or we would just go to his office. I knew he wasn't just a teacher; he was a man who truly cared about me. I was at a point where I had some hard decisions I had to make. Feelings were going to be hurt. I could have taken the easy way out. I was certainly tempted to do so at times. Ed listened and listened and listened. But in the end, he gave me that Hamlet moment that paved the way for every choice I'd have to make in life from there to eternity. He told me to be true to myself. I did and it wasn't easy. Twelve years later I'm still following Ed's advice and I'm blessed that it has led me to you.

Get to Work

The great football coach and mentor Lou Holtz defined a friend using three criteria: 1. Do they care about me? 2. Can I trust them? 3. Do they demand excellence from themselves? In order for us to get to work we really need to focus on numbers one and two. Certainly you want to be around people who demand excellence from themselves. If you spend your free time with troublemakers then you'll probably get in trouble. But you can demand the best from yourself while not giving your best to others. Care and trust are the key ingredients to being a good friend. If you care, then you will listen to the trials of your friend. If you're trustworthy, your friends will be able to reveal their innermost feelings to you. You might not think you're doing anything, but to your friend you are providing them with valuable therapy. I know you've heard the song "Lean on Me." Well, that's it. That's what friendship is all about. A friend provides shelter from the storm—hope in times of despair, courage in moments of fear, truth during days of deceit, peace in time of war, and love when faced with hate. Out of ten, how would you grade the friend you've been to others? Are you just a fairweather friend who only shows up when the sun is shining? Or, are you a faithful friend who is there even more on rainy days? Only you know the answer to these questions. How good of a friend has Jesus been to you? Don't you think we need to show the same love and friendship towards our earthly brothers and sisters? After all, it was Jesus who taught us that what we do to the least of those amongst us we do for Him. I pray that you have not become the world's definition of a friend. If you have then you've grown accustomed to giving all the wrong things to your friend, like material possessions. Now it's time to start becoming a friend like Jesus is to you. If you do what Jesus would do, then you'll realize that the greatest thing you can give your friend is your time.

Chapter 14 Uncle George

MAKE THE AMERICAN DREAM LIVE

My Uncle George graduated first in his high school class, went to college and then went on to medical school where he also graduated in the top percent and eventually operated his own medical practice for many years. He has a beautiful house, a beautiful wife and two great children, Andrew and Abigail. He has the luxury of eating at fancy restaurants, going on exotic vacations, driving fancy cars and sending his kids to the best schools. When I go to visit him I get treated like a king. He's worked hard and earned every penny he's spent. He's also earned the right to do what he chooses to do with his money. If he wants to build a fancy house away from the crime-infested city, then he has the right to do it. If he wants to drive an SUV that is a gas guzzler then that's his God given right. And he also has the right to choose what charities he wants to donate to and that also is his God given right. He's no beggar who's going to suck the taxpayer dry. He's a consumer and a proud contributor to our economy. He's the true definition of the American dream: hard work equals success. So why have people like my uncle been demeaned by the progressives and liberals in government? Why is the American dream shunned? Why are those making $225,000 a year or over penalized for their hard work through taxation without any representation? Why are they constantly told that they have to pay their fair share? Why? I'll tell you why. It's because the progressives and liberals in control of our country don't want to recognize our God given freedoms. They want to ensure their power by continually handing out freebies to those who refuse to work while taking off the backs of hard working Americans. This is socialism—or can even be called communism—and their goal is to attack every hardworking American who believes in their God given freedom. Jesus said that we should give to Caesar what belongs to Caesar. He didn't say we should give a good portion of our hard earned money to the government so politicians can get rich and embellish lavish benefit packages while others who refuse to work can live off the system. Last year alone I paid $16,000 in taxes and the majority of those are federal taxes. That number is downright appalling! I'll give you some more disturbing figures. According to the business magazine Forbes, 55% of people in our country do not pay taxes and 35% of people in the USA don't want to work. Did you hear these statistics? Over 50% don't pay taxes and 35% don't even want to work. Why should they have to work or pay taxes when they can freeload off the tax dollars of hard working Americans. I agree with President

Reagan who said that if you had two hands and two feet then you need to get a job. No job is beneath anyone. If you have to scrub floors or clean toilets then go out there and be the best floor scrubber and toilet cleaner money can buy. I got my start cleaning toilets and emptying garbage at the age of 14 for $3 an hour. God blessed me with the opportunity to clean toilets and empty garbage and I was grateful for every penny I earned. If you're called to do a dirty job then you should be grateful to. If you think this destruction of the American dream and work ethic and the attack on our God granted freedoms has all happened by accident then think again. This is a well crafted plan by socialists to destroy the American dream and to destroy our God given rights. So what can we do about it?

Get to Work

For starters we need to be very, and I mean very, educated voters. Just because a person represents a certain political party does not mean that they are a true conservative who believes in our God given rights. Do your research! There are many phonies in high places in Washington, D.C. Secondly, we need to encourage true conservatives with a backbone to run for office. They may have sound values, but if they have no integrity they need to be weeded out of the process. A person without a backbone will eventually be corrupted by the system. We need to find true public servants, not politicians. Politicians got us into this mess and a politician sure isn't going to get us out of it. We need leaders. We need a man like Jefferson Smith, the main character in the movie, *Mr. Smith Goes to Washington*, who are going to stand up to all the political bullies who want power and the socialists who desire to destroy the American dream. Thirdly, we need to push for a new tax code. My suggestion is a flat tax of 9%. Enough of this rigged system where cronies of big government along with those who live off the system get away with paying little or no taxes. It's the middle and upper class and small business owners that suffer with such an irrational system. Let me remind you, Jesus made the tax code pretty simple. He said give to Caesar what belongs to Caesar. He didn't exclude anybody. He didn't tell the Pharisees or high priests that they would be excluded since they were in the religious elite class. He didn't tell the poorer people they didn't have to pay taxes because they had a tough time finding work. He told everyone to pay their due. Everyone! So if we want to even out this tax problem, then we better make the 55% of people who aren't paying taxes start paying their equal amount. If we all enjoy the fruits of a free society then we should all be responsible for contributing to the system of a government that protects our liberties. Next, we need to train up our younger generation to be leaders. It's our job to mold the next George Washington and Ben Franklin amongst our youth. Lastly, we need to continue to live the American dream despite what the government says. We need to keep working hard and spending our money the best way we see fit. I do encourage you to support small businesses here in the USA because they are what make our economy flourish in the first place.

Now it's time to get to work. Be an educated voter, seek leaders, push for a flat tax where everyone pays, raise up leaders and continue to live the American dream. I'm confident that if every true American follows this practice then we will make the American dream live.

Chapter 15 Aunt Katie

YOUR SPOUSE IS
YOUR BEST FRIEND

"In good times, in bad times, I'm always on your side for evermore cause that's what friends are for, that's what friends are for." Those are the lines of a song from the 1980s. Those lines remind me so much of the relationship my Aunt Katie had with her late husband, Kevin. They were best friends. I loved being around them and seeing how closely they interacted with one another. They were inseparable. They truly defined what a marriage should be: a loving and growing relationship with your best friend. Although they were oftentimes together they both were aware how intricate a buffer zone was for their relationship. What I mean by a buffer zone is alone time apart from your spouse, doing things that you like to do. My uncle had the hobbies of working on cars in addition to working on house construction projects. In order for their relationship to thrive my aunt had to allow my uncle to do those things he enjoyed to do either by himself or with others. My aunt loved shopping so my uncle allowed her and my mom to go on shopping trips. It worked both ways and it made their marriage and friendship grow. I think if they were always around each other they might get on edge. Everyone needs a break; some free space away from the ones they love. It's only natural. Now I'm sure they had their disagreements, but what was it that truly made their marriage work? It was the love they had for each other and it was the fact that they were best friends. I saw love at its finest when my aunt took a sabbatical from work to take care of her dying husband. That's unconditional love. So where do you think this idea of husband and wife being best friends came from? I thought a husband and a wife were just supposed to love each other and everything would work out just fine. Let's take a look at where this idea of a spousal friendship came from.

Get to Work

I believe that we can learn all we need to know about a marriage from our very first parents, Adam and Eve. For the sake of brevity, I'm just going to focus on spousal friendship and how it had to exist between Adam and Eve. So let's hit the rewind button. God created Adam out of the dust of the earth, which he breathed life into. Then God created Eve by taking a part of Adam's rib. And that was it. He didn't create anybody else. Sure, there were the animals and nature, but there were no other living human beings. Only God was present to guide them and we all know how that worked out. With only two people living on the face of the earth, how could they possibly survive without being friends? They needed friendship to communicate on a daily basis. They needed friendship to figure out what they were going to eat and drink. They needed friendship to figure out how they were going to make shelter. They needed friendship to figure out how they were going to create and raise a family. Without friendship, they probably would have destroyed each other. So what does all of this mean for us? Well, this means that if you want your marriage to not only survive, but flourish, then your spouse needs to be your best friend. There is no other way around it. Let's go to the present. How are you going to run a household if your spouse is not your best friend? How are you going to raise children in a dark and evil world if your spouse is not your best friend? How are you going to get through tough times (and they will come) if your spouse is not your best friend? The answer: you won't. Marriages that have tried other remedies have failed. Marriages where a spouse is absent often have failed. Marriages where there is no teamwork have failed. Marriages where the husband is more worried about the football game score than taking his wife on a date night have failed. And your marriage will fail, too, if you don't get back to the very lesson the Lord taught us with our very first parents. God wrote out the gameplan for us. Follow it! When the pastor says, "'til death do us part" on the wedding day, he means that if this thing is going to go the long haul, spouses better be prepared to be best friends.

Maybe your marriage is suffering. Then it's time to get to work. Tell your spouse that you love them and you want to recommit your life to them. Then follow through with your words. Maybe you're in a serious relationship and marriage is right around the corner. I tell you this: next to the Lord, trust needs to be the center of your relationship now if you're going to be best friends in the future. Or maybe you're single and marriage is way off in the future. My best advice to you is that when you do meet a great companion, develop a friendship first. I made a big mistake by falling too quickly for a girl in the past. We were dating two months and were already talking about marriage. We didn't even get the chance to experience the joys of a fruitful friendship. When you get involved in a relationship, you should take it slow. Get to know each other first before you get serious. Remember what we learned from my Uncle Frank, "When you rush, accidents happen." Lastly, I am confident that if you follow the advice God gives us through the story of Adam and Eve, you will have a successful and bountiful marriage because your spouse will be your best friend.

Chapter 16: Fatherly Advice

Where have all the fathers gone? It's clearly evident in modern society that there are many children growing up in fatherless homes. The men of our society have "manned down" instead of "manned up". I'm not going to get into statistics here. Do the research for yourself and you will see what has happened to the family, especially the African American family since Lyndon Johnson waged his so called War on Poverty. Take a look at what has happened to families since entitlements like Welfare and Medicaid were instituted to fight this war on poverty. Marriage is also penalized in the Welfare system. It is encouraged that you have children out of wedlock to receive more Welfare benefits. Thank you, Lyndon Johnson! You singlehandedly waged a war that created more poverty and destroyed the union of marriage. If you think I'm kidding, then take a look at what has happened to the city of Detroit and what has happened to the number of children born into fatherless homes, especially amongst African Americans. Our government has destroyed fatherhood. Men would much rather hang out in bars, hook up with a woman than have a kid who they don't even acknowledge. And what about married men? How good of a job are they doing? They're more worried about watching the football game on Sunday than they are about taking their family to church and spending the day in fellowship. If you think I'm kidding, just take a look at what is happening to our Christian kids when they graduate high school. They are leaving the church in astounding numbers. Fathers are just like Adam; they are not leading. Adam should have been the man and leader and told his wife, Eve: "Whatever you do, don't eat of that tree." Instead, he let her fall. Men today are dropping the football just like Adam and are letting their wives and especially their children fall. This book is not meant to provide statistics. I have done the research and it's devastating. Just do a Google search on the "War on Poverty" and wait until you see what you find. If you want to research fatherhood, then I urge you to check out the Blaze TV online and watch a free video called Hutch and see the statistics this pastor has to give about fatherhood. If you think our kids being raised in churches are doing fine, then I urge you to check out the website of Josh McDowell and review his research.

I cannot think of a more beautiful thing to do with your life than to find the right woman, love her and raise godly children with her. Marriage and parenting is the greatest way to honor God, since we are His greatest creation. **ADD Moment: If you're an earther and you think we are not His greatest creation, then I would suggest**

you refresh your memory by reading Genesis. It has always been my desire to fall in love with a beautiful, godly woman, get married and have children. God is still urging me to be patient with this passion and He may do the same for you when you get older. After all, who you marry will be the biggest decision you'll ever make next to whether or not you choose Jesus as your savior. It's easy to change a job or change an address. It's not easy to change your wife or husband. It's against God's law to change your wife or husband just because you want to. God lays out certain grounds for divorce and sadly our society has not followed them. And, if you have kids, you can't exchange them for something else. So, even though I'm not a father yet, it is still my God-given responsibility to show fatherly love to all those I meet along the way. God has given me the duty of being a role model, whether I like it or not. The duty to teach and live the Ten Commandments rests on my shoulders and on the backs of all men in this world. Honestly, I feel honored with the opportunity to set a positive example for someone else. I've been around a time or two before and I've taught and coached both young adults and adults. This next section is my attempt, through the grace of God, to provide some fatherly advice to people who live in a cruel world—a cruel world that exploits impressionable persons who come from fatherless homes every day.

Chapter 17: Fatherly Advice #1

GIRLS + GUYS + HORMONES + BOOZE = TROUBLE

I am by no means a math person. But, if there is one equation I know it's the one mentioned above. As Willie Nelson once sang, "The nightlife ain't no good life, but it's my life." From experience, that lyric is 100% true. The ingredients present in a barroom, in a club, at a sporting event or at a concert are a recipe for disaster. If students in a chemistry lab started mixing random chemicals in the wrong way, then something would eventually blow up. That's the nightlife in a nutshell. The wrong ingredients are being mixed in the wrong manner, which eventually leads to an explosion. What are examples of an all out blow up? Some examples are a fist fight, a one night stand, a relationship starting with lust, a pregnancy and drinking and driving, just to name a few. All of these have horrible consequences and are a very real possibility when you mix the equation's ingredients. Girls, guys and hormones will always be present. The one ingredient that ignites the fire is most certainly booze.

The last time I checked, alcohol didn't make anyone smarter. But the last time I checked booze certainly causes someone to act in a manner that is not rational or consistent with their normal behavior. People don't drink to prepare for a test. They don't drink in the morning to wake up for work. And people don't drink to improve the health of their body. So why then do people desire to drink? I would contend that most people drink to numb the pain or fill a void that has been left in their life. The booze makes them feel happy in a place that is normally empty. The booze makes someone forget about an internal pain. Many others might booze because it's part of the culture's tradition here in America. I had my first drink at the age of fifteen. After a basketball game we picked up a local known for getting beer for young kids. We then went to a baseball field and I drank a 40 oz bottle of Budweiser. I felt great! I felt like I was flying. I was laughing, feeling loopy, singing and having a good time. It was awesome! I woke up in the morning and still felt a bit dizzy, but all I could remember was how awesome of a night I had. Although I thought it was awesome, it was just a night to numb the emptiness inside of me. When I woke up in the morning the emptiness was still there, but now I found something to look forward to that would fill the void: booze. I couldn't wait until the next time I got drunk. Let's just say that there were ten more years of next times. When I got older and realized that good looking girls partied, too I was even more hooked. At all the parties and in all the clubs and barrooms I was hoping to meet the right girl who I could commit to. Well, that never happened. I met many of the wrong girls, but never met the girl I was going to take home to mom. As I sit back and reflect, I cannot think of one good thing that booze led to. I could tell you all of the negative things, but then I'd have to write another book for that one. The best positive is that I can tell you my story and pray that people listen.

Sadly, we live in a society whereby commercialism targets the college students and older single people, since they are so impressionable. The nightlife is the cool thing to do. Getting drunk, acting stupid and randomly hooking up with another girl/guy is the norm. If you're going out to a movie and dinner with your family on a Friday night, then there must be something wrong with you. The nightlife scene is not a good place to be, but it is especially dangerous for young women. I've been blessed to work security and as a bouncer in numerous clubs and venues. I've been involved in many fights, had a knife pulled on me twice, been sprayed with mace and so on. But, as a sober observer, the most disturbing thing I've seen has been women who are treated like an object. Young women—the nightlife in a bar is not a good place to be, unless you want to hookup with the wrong guy. Most guys have the wrong thing on their mind when it comes to girls. Drunk guys most certainly have the wrong thing on their mind when it comes to women. Girls, don't be a victim of a guy who wants to use you to fulfill his own lustful desires. And guys, get your acts together. Think of someone acting in such a way towards your sister or mother. What would you do if you observed them being taken advantage of in a lustful way? I hope and pray that this thought will help you break the addiction of lust.

My fatherly advice is to seek happiness by being around good company in a good place. If you are a firm believer and have gotten a little off track in the nightlife, then I would advise you to spend more time with your family and Christian friends. Watch and discuss a Christian movie over the weekend. Go to a Christian concert. Attend a singles class. Start a Bible study with your friends. Ask your local pastor for help if you're struggling to put the wheels in motion. If you haven't accepted Jesus Christ as your Lord and Savior, then I pray that you make that choice right now. I've lived the hard road where I tried to find fulfillment in a bottle or a lustful desire. In the end I woke up with the same emptiness and pain, but on top of it I also had a hangover. It is only He who can remove you from a life of gluttony and lust. It is only He who can replace the pain with peace through His love rather than a bottle of whisky. It is only He who can fill the void of loneliness in your life with friendship through His grace rather than a one night stand. I pray that the Lord is allowing these words to work through you right now. Let the healing and rebirth begin because girls + guys + hormones + booze = trouble.

Chapter 18: Fatherly Advice #2

TELL YOUR SIGNIFICANT OTHER THEY ARE THE CLEANUP HITTER

It's so easy for young, rambunctious teenagers and even adults to get their priorities mixed up. Sometimes they even become obsessed with the priorities at the top of their list, which usually aren't the right ones. That top priority for many is their significant other. This will only lead to ruination; the ruination of a fine student, athlete and young man/woman. Blood pressures will rise when the relationship gets rocky. Grades will drop when your boyfriend drops you. Bad habits will take form as your boyfriend/girlfriend becomes the center of your life. Arguments will occur with parents. Rules will be broken. Your parents will need a daily dose of Pepto-Bismol when they realize how much in love you are. Most importantly it will lead to the ruination of one's spiritual walk with the Lord for those who are firm believers. For the unbelievers, it will only pull them further away from knowing the peace that comes from being cleansed by the Lord's grace. Folks, here's the good news: it happens to the majority of teenagers and adults at one time or another.

The girl I dated my junior year in high school was at the top of my lineup. She was actually my good friend's ex-girlfriend. That was my first mistake. I was a good athlete and that year I ran track for the first time. I was very successful in the long jump and was seeded high at the district meet. My dream of winning a medal didn't happen. Ruination took control instead. You see, the relationship went south and I got all worked up because my #1 took herself out of the lineup all together. Strike three. I was out. I did horrible at the district meet considering the fact that I was mentally out of it. Now do you see what ruination will do? Here's the bottom line: chances are that you aren't going to marry your high school sweetheart. Chances are your heart will be broken at least once. Chances are that you will get plenty of second chances with the Lord. But, first off, you need to get your life lineup in order.

Let me clear up the misconception here. In baseball, the most powerful hitter is usually the cleanup hitter or the fourth person in the lineup. Just because your boyfriend or girlfriend is going to be the cleanup hitter in your lineup doesn't mean they are the best hitter. In fact they are behind three really important hitters. Here's the standard lineup for a young person: 1. The Lord 2. Family 3. Work/School and Goals. Let's take a look at these in greater detail.

If I were to draw a picture of a circle and a cross, where would you put the cross? Outside the circle? On the edge of the circle? In the middle of the circle? The middle of the circle is where it should be, which would symbolize that Christ is the center of your life. There's no other way it can work. If the Lord is not the center of your life, then you will replace Him with worldly things, which will always let you down. Having Christ as the center of your life means that you will have a personal relationship with Him. It's His love through His death that will provide you with serenity and allow you to live fully in your relationship with others while enjoying work and the pursuit of goals.

Often times teenagers and even adults don't want to be around their family. They'd rather be hanging out with friends. Children have an obligation to obey and help their parents. God even commanded to Moses that children should obey thy mother and father. Obeying means that you do what your parents tell you to do in a respectful manner. I would think many teenagers or adults still living at home have the "doing" thing down pat; however, the respectful manner aspect is probably a struggle. Teenagers and young, single adults are at an age where it's common to rebel. They're naturally going to rebel against the two people who have been enforcing rules with them since day one. The easiest way to do that is through disrespect. My father always used to say to me that I was "untouchable". What he meant was that I was going to do my thing all the time and listen to nobody, not even my parents. He was 100% right. I was untouchable. I did my chores and what not, however I rarely showed my parents the respect they deserved. Secondly, teenagers and young, single adults also have the responsibility to help their parents. If your father needs you to cut the grass, then you better drop whatever you are doing to help him cut the grass. Cutting the grass is a small task compared to the help your parents provide for you through food, clothing, shelter and finances. It's not cheap to raise a family. The least you can do is help around the house to show your appreciation. Maintaining a household is a daily job for parents. It's not at all easy. Help them before it's too late. Think about this for a minute: one day your parents will get old and not be able to take care of their household. Are you going to be prepared to help them take care of the house you were raised in? God tells us that it is our duty. Stop being untouchable! Realign your lineup and move your parents to the #2 spot. Trust me. They certainly have you near the top of theirs.

School work and goals are critical to take seriously if you desire to be successful and a provider for your future family. It's difficult enough to find a good job even if you have good grades. It's nearly impossible if you are just getting by or if your grades are very poor. It's essential to develop good habits when you are younger. One of the best habits you can develop is studying every single night. If you are accustomed to preparing every day for school, then it will be much easier to make the transition to college and the workplace when the workload will heavily increase. Having goals is also very important for your well being. Your goals may deal with athletics, music, art, speech/debate, earning a scholarship, getting a promotion, etc. The bottom line is that there is only one way to achieve your goals—through hard work. What separates the good from the great in any field is work ethic. The good student just relies on their intelligence. The great student relies on their work ethic to achieve success. Those who achieve excellence in their goals work hard all the time, even when they are on top of the mountain. They don't sleep in or take any days off. After all, the word "success" only comes before work in the dictionary. If you desire to be a good student who accomplishes goals outside of the classroom, then you better be spending more time working than talking to your significant other on the phone.

Your spiritual and domestic fulfillment comes down to a simple choice: ruination or dedication. If you want to experience ruination with the Lord, your family and your schoolwork and goals, then you can continue to spend more time with your "gf" or "bf". On the other hand, if you strive to feel the peace and enjoy the fruits life has to offer, then you need to dedicate your time to the Lord, your family and schoolwork and goals. I'd choose option "B". If you do the same, then be prepared to tell your "love bug" that they are the new cleanup hitter in your lineup.

Chapter 19: Fatherly Advice #3

#1 IS THE ONLY NUMBER THAT EVER MATTERS

Let's talk about pride and protection. America used to be a place where pride really mattered. People took pride in doing their best at everything they did. We wanted to make the best cars, build the biggest schools, draft the finest army and create the best workers. With the exception of our armed forces, America is lagging behind other countries. Let's be honest, we're not falling behind, we're getting our butts kicked. Our automobile industry is in the gutter with the exception of Ford. **ADD Moment: They did not accept any bailout money.** Our schools are constantly outperformed by other countries like Japan. Lastly, our workers are turning into lazy nincompoops thanks to Medicaid, welfare and food stamps. **ADD Moment: Over 40 million people are on food stamps. In a free republic there should not be one person receiving food stamps.** What do we have to protect if we are no longer #1 in performance?

Satan is going to go after those he doesn't have. He wants to knock people off the top. He wants to take a Christian and bring them down and away from the Lord. He's only going to go after those who are doing well. I'm no statistician, but I would argue that most Christians are successful in their given fields. For those who have fallen on hard times, I would contend that they are relying on their faith and church to provide rather than the government. Satan's going to tempt those who are on fire for the Lord. He's not going to tempt those who are living off the government and enjoying a seven day weekend. He has no reason to attack free loaders, which is why they live such carefree and apathetic lives. Satan doesn't have to go after those he already has. Since we've allowed ourselves to become lazy nincompoops across the board in America, we no longer have anything to protect.

How do we get our pride back? First, let me direct believers who are on track with the Lord. *You simply need to provide a hand up to people rather than a hand out.* You need to encourage and empower them to provide for themselves. Secondly, you need to be a well trained and obedient voter. To vote, you need to be obedient to God's word and commands. You need to elect public servants who support personal responsibility rather than the creation of a welfare state. Nonbelievers simply need to get right with the Lord. If you are used to being slackers, drifters and dependant on others to provide for you, then it's time to take out the firehouse, spray yourself down and wake up. Enough is enough! God didn't make you to be a lazy nincompoop. He gave you a mind to think and a body to work. Now, get to it! Get right first with the Lord and he will make your days more fulfilling when you get into His word and His work. You will feel very refreshed when you're able to provide for yourself rather than rely on others. Get to work!

Next, how do we protect ourselves from the fiery darts of the wicked one? We simply need to stay in the word and in fellowship with believers. We cannot go off on an island by ourselves. When that happens, we are likely to be overcome with pride and get away from His word and fellowship. The Dark One hates scripture because it's God's word. We need to arm ourselves with scripture on a daily basis. Fellowship is key. We need to share our joys and struggles with believers. If you're not in a Bible study class, then get in one as soon as possible. We need to share scripture and pray with fellow believers. Where two or three are gathered in the name of the Lord, He is in their midst. That's power. Arming yourself with scripture and fellowship is throwing a barrage of potent punches at Satan. He stands no chance of defending himself and we stand every chance of gaining victory with the Lord while enjoying the fruits of his blessings.

In sum, the world is going to tell you to relax, take it easy and live free. The world will tell you to let someone else take care of you. Shut the devil up and listen to the Lord, because the number one is the only number that really matters.

Chapter 20: Fatherly Advice #4

FIND A PLACE WHERE YOUR MIND AND HEART INTERSECT

Jesus wants everyone to be at peace. Obviously we are going to be at peace during times of prayer, scripture reading and fellowship. But how can we find peace when we are trapped in a loud and disturbing world? The only way to find peace outside of our relationship with God is by finding a place where our mind and heart connect. If we just used our minds to find peace then we would be wrapped in theory. Our decisions would be textbook answers. We would be like trained robots spewing out information without any emotions. If we just used our heart or emotions to make decisions, then we'd be wrapped in high blood pressure. We would come across as emotional train wrecks. We'd be really angry if someone upset us or really happy if something made us excited. We need a break. We all desire to have serenity in our lives, yet we don't know how to get there. Our minds and hearts are at a constant battle when in the world. They are so fragile and so imperfect. When are we supposed to come up with a thought-filled answer? When are we supposed to make a decision based on emotions? Living with impressionable minds and hearts is a psychological battle. We have to retrain ourselves to let the battle go, to surrender. Surrendering does not mean we are giving up. It means we are putting the Lord in complete control. Here's how to do it.

First, we must recognize that the world is cruel. If we recognize that worldly things are cruel, then we can learn how to separate ourselves from them. If you're a true Christian, people should perceive you as different. If you find yourself around worldly people, then you need to distinguish who you are through your fruits. Secondly, we must recognize that our minds and emotions are very imperfect when we rely on ourselves. If we just ran with the thoughts in our heads or in our hearts, we'd be in turmoil. Thirdly, once we understand that the world is cruel and that we have flawed minds and emotions, then we need to rely on someone for help. That someone is the only one, the Lord and Savior Jesus Christ. Lastly, the only way to rely on Him is to surrender our lives, our minds and our emotions to Him. By doing so, we will take every thought and every emotion in captivity to Christ. The outcome is that we will be more Christ- minded and Christ-hearted. What a beautiful thing to be considered like Christ. When we surrender, we will no longer have to worry about straining our minds to make a decision. When we surrender, we will no longer have to worry about getting worked up about a situation. Before we think and before we feel, we will be trained at knowing that Jesus holds us in the very palm of His hands. I can't think of any thought or emotion that is more peaceful. Let me tell you of a time of complete serenity with the Lord.

    I was struggling internally. I found myself falling into old habits and ways of thinking. I missed worship because I chose not to go. I felt the Lord could not forgive me for getting off track. It was a cloudy day and I just felt the need to pray. I was going to lay it all on the line with the Lord with the way I was feeling. I asked the Lord for forgiveness. I was sitting at my desk with my eyes closed. I held out my palms in prayer. And then I felt this brightness and warm feeling. The phrase, "Come with me my son" kept repeating in my mind. I closed my hands and grabbed hold of the Lord. My hands started to shake as I made this choice. Satan certainly didn't want this to occur. I opened my eyes and guess what happened? The clouds broke and the sun came out. I felt at such peace knowing that I was in the Lord's hands. He called me "his son" like a loving father. He spoke in such a calm and peaceful voice. His presence was so serene and soothing. He didn't yell or shout at me to follow Him. He didn't show any anger because I had gotten off track with Him. The Lord's grace is such a peaceful and cleansing feeling. That's what He wants us to feel all the time. How do we do it?

    I've given you some instructions on the mindset we need to have. Once that mindset becomes part of our repertoire, we simply need to seek His face. Trust me—from experience, it is the peaceful face of a loving and heavenly father. Remember that He is calling you His son and daughter. Remember that He has His hands held out for us to hold on to. Surrender, seek His face and you will come to a place of complete peace, a place where your mind and heart intersect.

Chapter 21: Fatherly Advice #5

LEAVE THE BAGGAGE DRAGGING BEHIND AND MOVE FORWARD

Often times we are burdened by our past. We dwell on mistakes, missed opportunities, failed relationships and fail to move forward. When we focus on the past, we become "I wishers". I wish I did this. I wish I did that. We could easily wish our lives away worrying about the things we cannot control. The biggest thing we cannot control that we want to control is the past. There's a reason why they call it the past, because it has already passed. It's gone. It's over and done with. Oh, but how our minds work that they can easily take us back to the place we used to be. If you're living in the past, then you're a baggage dragger. Imagine going to the airport. We've all been there before where we see the guy who has three bags around his shoulders, two in his hands and another clenched in his teeth. And he has two kids trying to drag them along. And he's trying really hard to run, but he keeps on hitting the bags. The kids are falling behind and he's getting upset. He's a sweaty mess from all the work. The worst part is that he misses his flight to an all inclusive Caribbean resort. If you're living in the past, then that guy is you, the baggage dragger. He can't get to the beautiful place he wants to go because he has too much baggage. Now here's the other guy. He has one bag around his shoulders. He's holding two kids in his hands. He's walking with a laid back pace and he's smiling brightly because he knows he has nothing to worry about. Now, who do you want to be? Do you want to be the baggage dragger who misses his flight and his dream vacation? Or do you want to be the calm, cool and collected guy who doesn't have a worry in the world because he knows he and his kids are going to reach their destination? The choice is yours: baggage drag or move forward.

Here's the truth: whether you believe it or not, God has a beautiful plan for your life. The only way you will ever get to experience His plans for your life is to let go of your past and move forward. If you continue to baggage drag, you will never get to see the beautiful places and experience the beautiful plans the Lord has for you. You'll be like the guy at the airport who misses his dream vacation because he's hauling too much luggage around. I know you're saying that leaving the baggage behind is tough. You're going to tell me, "I've done so much wrong." "I've made so many mistakes." "My life will never be the same due to the choices I made." You've even convinced yourself that you cannot move forward. Stop believing the lies that Satan keeps telling you. It's time to shut him up. Here's how we're going to do it.

First, you need to seek forgiveness. Whatever you did wrong or whatever was not good enough in the past, you need to ask God to forgive you for those burdens. Forgiveness is a free gift only if you truly believe that Jesus Christ died for your sins. Forgiveness can only come from the blood of Jesus. There is absolutely no earthly way that exists that is capable of cleansing you from past sins. The Lord is the only way. Secondly, you need to repent from your old ways. Seeking forgiveness is the emotional solution to the problem. Repentance is the physical part of the solution. Repenting from old ways is going to be a ton of work. Satan wants you to repeat the recycle of old habits. The Lord wants you to move forward and be the real you. A spiritual battle will occur between the devil and the Lord. If you put your trust in the Lord and arm yourself with scripture and prayer, Satan's attempts to hijack your life will be defeated. Repentance is going to be challenging. There will be days that you will slip and stumble. But just remember who is capable of holding you up: the Lord. If you fall down, immediately seek forgiveness from the Lord.

Here's the bottom line: any good thought comes from the Lord and anything negative comes from Satan. Jesus does not tempt us; Satan does. So, when you feel like the luggage man at the airport, then you know that it is Satan who's trying to weigh you down. When this occurs, seek help from the Lord. When you feel like the calm, cool and collected traveler, then give thanks to the Lord for taking away your burdens. Remember, if you follow the Lord step for step, you will leave the baggage dragging behind and move forward.

Chapter 22: Fatherly Advice #6
ANALYZE, ADAPT AND ACHIEVE

You may remember the name Vince Papale. Maybe I'm wrong. I bet you remember the name of the movie *Invincible*. I had the privilege of meeting Mr. Papale at a coaching clinic a few years back. He told us his life lessons and story, which is identical to the movie that portrayed his life. He hit a really tough time in his life in his mid twenties. His wife left him. He lost his teaching job. He had to move back with his father. His life was headed on a one way street to nowhere. Isn't it awesome how God presents us with opportunities in the midst of our most difficult struggles? Well, God did that for Vince. The Philadelphia Eagles held an open tryout for anyone interested in trying to make the team. New coach Dick Vermeil tried to put a spark in the team with the open tryout. Vince was really down on his luck and as a good athlete it was time for him to analyze, adapt and achieve.

Vince didn't panic when his life was falling apart. He didn't drown himself in his sorrows. He first analyzed the problem. He knew there was nothing he could do about losing his wife and his job. An opportunity presented itself thanks to the Lord and Vince went to work to get himself in shape for the tryout. That's analyzing. Next, he had to adapt. Vince had to get used to a new lifestyle. He had no wife, no job and he had to move back in with his father. He adapted by setting up a training schedule and taking care of his mind and body in order to prepare for the tryout. Adapting for him required great effort. Lastly, he achieved. Vince achieved by making the Philadelphia Eagles team and becoming a viable player on their special teams. Analyze, adapt and achieve. How are you going to do so when life throws you a few knockout punches like it did to Mr. Papale?

In the midst of our most difficult times, God is telling us that he loves us. The Lord is telling us that we need to completely rely on him instead of trying to overcome obstacles on our own. If we seek Him during these tough times, He will help us to analyze, adapt and achieve. He wants us to get back on track with our lives. He wants to pick us up in the middle of our struggles. But he cannot fulfill his promise for our lives if we give into our own desires of anger and self-pity while turning our hearts cold. If we give into the flesh, Satan will take us on a highway to hell. At our weakest point, Satan can really wreak havoc in our lives, which is why we need to continue to trust and seek the Lord. When you are down and out, the Lord will have your back. You need to believe that He will protect you if you want to analyze, adapt and achieve.

Chapter 23: Fatherly Advice #7

YOU ARE BLESSED TO DO GREAT THINGS

Do you realize that you were put on this earth by God for a purpose? Do you realize that you have certain God-given talents, which are to be used to fulfill His purpose for your life and the furtherance of His kingdom here on earth? Do you realize that you were born to do great things rather than just be an average person drifting along? Do you realize that God knew you before you were even created? Do you realize that the Lord God molded you with his own two hands? Do you realize that He has all the hairs on your head numbered? Aren't you just blown away by this reality? If God created you with his own two hands, from your head to toes, from your heart to soul, don't you think he has great plans for you to do big things with your life? If not, then think about this. Walt Disney created Disney World and the Disney dynasty. He once said, "If you could dream it, you could do it. Just remember this whole thing started with a mouse." When Walt Disney had that vision of a mouse, don't you think he had big plans for that mouse once it was created? When he created Disney World, don't you think he saw big things happening? When Henry Ford built the Model T, don't you think he had a big vision for the thing he created? Take a look at what Disney and Ford have become. They are two of the biggest and most successful companies in the world and it all started with a vision and a creation. Your life began in just the same way, with a vision and a creation. There's just one big difference: your Creator is not Walt Disney or Henry Ford, it's the Almighty, All Powerful and All Loving, the Lord Jesus Christ. Wow! Think of what could become of your life with the knowledge of who your Creator is. Your Creator defied death, so imagine what you could do with your life. Nothing is beyond His power or limitations.

At the same coaching clinic where I met Vince Papale, I happened to meet the wide receiver of the Philadelphia Eagles, Jason Avant, at the Fellowship of Christian Athletes breakfast. His testimony was so powerful and such a tribute to the plans the Lord has for your life, no matter what your background is. Jason Avant grew up in a poor, fatherless home in the city of Chicago. He and his brothers and sisters lived in a small house. The only room for him to sleep was in his bed with his grandmother. He was tied up with the wrong crowd. The road he was headed on was going to either lead him to jail or death. Each night when he would try to sleep, he would hear his grandmother praying for him. In high school a mentor got Jason to go out for the football team. He was just a practice player until one day when a coach approached him. The coaches knew Jason's background and they just tried to do all they could to help him. One coach came over to Jason at practice, grabbed Jason's hands and started rubbing holy oil over them. He said, "Jason, from now on, your hands are anointed." Jason ended up getting the opportunity to play wide receiver for his high school team. By the time he was a senior, he was the best receiver in the state of Illinois. He earned a scholarship to play for Michigan and was drafted by the Eagles, where he is a current key player for the team. Jason told us that every time a ball is thrown to him, whether it is a drop or a catch, he lifts his hands in the air to give praise to his savior, Jesus Christ and the coach who saw that Jason was blessed to do great things. His testimony was so powerful and such a reminder to me of the plans God has for us. The most special thing about these plans is that we will be given the opportunity to use our talents to bless the lives of others just like Jason is doing.

Folks, there are countless Jason Avant stories out there. Maybe yours is similar. Just close your eyes for a second and imagine what the Lord can do with your life. Imagine the blessings he has in store for you. Imagine that his plans are even greater than the dreams you have for your life. If you truly believe in the Lord, you will realize that you are no wallflower; instead you are blessed to do great things.

Chapter 24: Fatherly Advice #8

LOVE IS THE ONLY PACKAGE YOU CAN'T LEAVE BEHIND

In November 2001 I went to a U2 concert in Philadelphia. It was probably the most emotional concert I ever attended. It was two months after September 11th and people were still feeling the reeling effects. Throughout the concert images would appear throughout the arena. There was one image that caught my attention. The image was a suitcase with a heart on the inside. I immediately began to wonder what that heart symbolized. I did my research and the name of U2's album was *All That You Can't Leave Behind*. That was it! Your heart, your love was all that you couldn't leave behind on your travels. So, how do we remember to keep our heart with us everywhere we go?

Do you realize the impact that you can make in the life of somebody else? Do you know that your presence can change or even save a life? We travel each and every day. We go from home to work, from home to school, from home to the store, and from home to the gym, etc. In these travels we are always meeting people. Some of them are complete strangers that we will never see again. Some are those we see on a regular basis. But we still have the ability to make an impact on their lives. That's if we are taking our love and our hearts with us. When we travel we can forget to take our briefcase to a meeting. We can forget our toothpaste and brush when we go on vacation. It's not going to be the end of the world if we forget a material possession. But the one thing we can never forget is our love for the Lord, our love for the life he has blessed us with and our love for each other. That is the only package that you can never leave behind.

Love cannot cure an illness. A smile cannot change the score on a failing test. A simple "hello" cannot heal a broken heart. But let me tell you something, it sure can help. If we carry the Lord's love in our heart each and every day, then we are going to see a visible impact made in the lives of others. Love is contagious and needed in the lives of everybody. We have no idea what's going on in a person's life. That "hello" or smile might be the only nice gesture that person will receive in a day. Just imagine how good you might make them feel. In the city of Houston there was this traffic cop known for bringing a smile to peoples' lives. He would dance, smile and do all sorts of funny things when he directed traffic. People going to work would purposefully change their routes just to see this man perform. I don't know whether this man was a Christian, but I do know that he was showing the love the Lord has for him and the love he has for others by his actions.

Folks, there is absolutely no force or weapon that is as powerful as the love that is inside of your heart. Don't bury it! Release it! Let the Lord do His work with your love. Let Him use you as a conduit to pour blessings into the lives of others. It may be through a smile, a friendly "hello", a much-needed conversation for someone in need, or through a holding of the door for an old lady at the grocery store. Let the Lord sing a song to your soul that you will sing to the entire world. You will sing a song to the world in your travels. They will see and feel your heart. Travel on and pour out the Lord's love for the world, because love is the only package that you can never leave behind.

Conclusion

THE BEGINNING IS NEAR

I normally would say that the end is near. That would seem appropriate since this is the end of our reading. However, this just marks the beginning of the *Lifework Guide to Happiness*. Please take out the hand you were assigned to trace at the beginning of the *Lifework Guide*. Now I want you to go to your favorite quiet place where you will be able to reflect. In your pinky, ring and middle finger, I would like you to write three words that describe you. In your pointer finger, write a goal that you have for the week. In your thumb, write a goal you have one month from now. In your palm, write a goal that you would like to accomplish one year from now. Lastly, draw a star above your hand and write a life goal. If there is one thing you want to accomplish, what is it? Maybe you want to be a doctor. Or maybe you just want to get married and have kids.

Do you realize that there is not one other person on this planet who has the same hand as you? Do you realize that there is not a single person in the world who would do this activity exactly like yourself? Do you realize that there is only one you in this entire world? Only one. Isn't that thought absolutely amazing? What you wrote in your hand and in the star is who you are, both inside and out. There is no other replica of you on mother Earth. So, who created this unique individual with special qualities and little weekly goals leading to yearly goals, leading to life goals? Such a special and amazing person could only have been created by such an amazing, miraculous and loving God—the Lord and Savior Jesus Christ.

If you read this book, maybe your wheels are turning about this whole Jesus thing. Well, let me turn them a little more. Maybe it's been a long time since you last went to church. Maybe the church you attended was dominated by a strict adherence to rules and tradition. Maybe you feel like you've done too much wrong and that there is no way God could possibly forgive you. Maybe you have never heard of who Jesus really is until you read this book. Or maybe you used to walk closely to the Lord, but then you got off track. Well let's put all of the past behind so you can pay attention to a few questions that will probably change your life. Do you admit that you're a sinner? Do you know that only Jesus can save you from your sins? Do you believe that Jesus gave His precious blood and that He died on the cross to pay for your sins? Do you believe that Jesus was buried in a tomb and three days later He came alive again, never to die, but to live forever? Do you believe that God loves you so very much? Do you believe that He has a plan for your life? Now,

I'm going to ask you the one question that will change your life forever: do you want to accept Jesus as your personal Savior? If you do, God promises you a brand new life. He will turn the darkness into light and wipe you clean of all your sins. He promises you life right now and life forever with Him in heaven. If you want to accept Jesus as your Lord and Savior, I'm going to ask you to confess this prayer with your whole heart: "Dear heavenly Father, I admit that I have lived a sinful life. I believe that you gave your precious blood and died on the cross for my sins. But I believe that You didn't stay dead. You were buried in a tomb and came alive again three days later. I ask you to forgive me of my sins. I want to accept you as my Lord and Savior. I ask you to come and live in my heart. I love you, Lord Jesus. Thank you! In Jesus's name, amen." If you said that prayer with your whole heart, I would like to welcome you to the family of God. I encourage you to grow in your faith by finding a Bible teaching church. Find Christian friends. Read your Bible daily. Pray daily. And most importantly, tell others what the Lord Jesus has done for you.

Now it's time to take your hand and love for the Lord and plan to begin your *Lifework Guide to Happiness*. Take hold of the Lord's hand and allow Him to take you on a journey that's going to be amazing. Spread your wings and fly with the Lord. At times you may seem to be falling, but just remember that with the Lord we will always have a parachute and safe landing zone. You are in His grip.

I want to thank you for coming along with me on this special journey. It is my prayer that the Lord continues to bless your life. It is my prayer that the Lord uses you as an instrument to have an impact on the lives of others. It is my prayer that your love for the Lord penetrates the lives of others. May the good Lord continue to bless you and keep you well because the beginning is near.

As Ever, On Eagle's Wings,
Christopher M. Kasian